PRAY WITH YOUR EYES OPEN

Looking at God, Ourselves, and Our Prayers

Richard L. Pratt, Jr.

Presbyterian and Reformed Publishing Company
Phillipsburg, New Jersey

Manufactured in the United States of America.

Library of Congress Cataloging-in-Publication Data

Pratt, Richard L., 1953–
   Pray with your eyes open.

   1. Prayer. I. Title.
BV215.P74   1987   248.3′2   87–2762
ISBN 0-87552-377-3
ISBN 0-87552-378-1 (pbk.)

To

Dick Ayers
Dick Chewning
Frank Crane
and
Bob Vincent

precious fathers and brothers
whose prayers have sustained me
through times of need.

Contents

Preface

This book is about prayer—one of our greatest blessings and one of our biggest struggles. Everywhere I go, believers share the same burden. We know instinctively that prayer is essential to the Christian life, and we search for help in this area. But we constantly face the inadequacies of our prayer lives. How can we improve our prayers? What can we do to make communication with God more central and more fulfilling? This book searches for answers to those questions.

As the title indicates, the central theme of these chapters is that we must learn to pray with our eyes open. I do not mean our physical eyes, but the eyes of our hearts. We need to examine what we think, do, and feel in prayer. All too often we approach communication with God with little reflection. Our habits take over and we are left to the mercy of patterns that have never been examined. In this book we will take a hard look at several important dimensions of Christian prayer.

After the foundational perspectives of chapter 1, the book is divided into three major parts. Part One (chaps. 2 through 5) investigates how to focus more carefully on God in prayer. Part Two (chaps. 6 through 9) searches for ways in which we may look more effectively at ourselves as we talk with God. Part Three (chaps. 10 through 13) looks directly at how we may improve our communication skills in prayer. Chapter 14 offers some closing suggestions on putting the content of the book into action. This format is designed for the quarter system used in many small-group studies and church schools.

This is not a book to be read in one sitting. Readers will benefit the most if they *practice* the content of a chapter before moving on to the next. Each chapter ends with questions and exercises designed to help readers incorporate the content into their lives. My strong suggestion is that readers study one chapter per week and spend some time through the week practicing what they have learned.

This book deals with only a few dimensions of prayer. It offers no magical formulas; it promises no full resolution of problems. It does reflect, however, nearly ten years of my own search for a more satisfying and God-honoring prayer life. That search certainly continues; I have not arrived. Yet, my hope is that the probings of this book will encourage others to join in the pilgrimage of prayer, a journey whose end will come only when we meet God face to face.

Richard L. Pratt, Jr.
Reformed Theological Seminary

Acknowledgments

This book has certainly been a team effort. Many thanks go to Gena, my wife, who has been a faithful sounding board as we have implemented this material in our own prayer lives. Much recognition is due to John Farrar, whose generous help and support have made this project a reality. Special gratitude is extended to Janet Miller, whose tireless processing of the manuscript and daily encouragement in the office have been indispensable. Many thanks also go to Becky Hobbs and Patty Brown for their fine editorial work. To my student assistants Bill Gleason, Steve Rarig, Greg Perry, and Tom Cannon, I offer my sincere appreciation for countless hours devoted to this project. Finally, I am grateful to my friends at Reformed Theological Seminary who have used this material and offered constructive suggestions while it was in the making.

1

The Problem With Prayer

Lord, till I reach yon blissful shore,
No privilege so dear shall be
As thus my inmost soul to pour
In prayer to thee.
                    Charlotte Elliott
                    1789–1871

He'd done it again. For the third time in five minutes he'd wandered off the track—so far off, in fact, that he couldn't even remember where he'd been. Pulling himself upright and adjusting the bed sheets around him, he thought it ridiculous that he should have such a problem—absolutely inexcusable. At no time in his life had prayer come easily. Now with eyes clenched shut, he grieved, "Hard to believe I've been a Christian for ten years, and still I have to force myself to pray."

Many Christians experience this same frustration in their prayer lives. New believers, mature Christians, pastors, famous evangelists—no group is exempt. Many great leaders would be embarrassed to admit their lack of success with prayer. And so it is with most of us. We know that prayer is one of the greatest blessings God offers, but we also know that it is a source of frustration and guilt. Stories that tell of dramatic answers to prayer set our hearts yearning for the same. A life filled with prayer is a life of great blessing. But such fulfillment seems to come to only a few.

The rest of us, crippled by frustration, simply put prayer out of our lives. Hectic schedules and demanding responsibilities push

1

conversation with God into the dark and dusty corners of our lives. When we slip in a word of prayer now and then, we cannot help but sense how shallow it is. This harsh reality raises a number of questions: Can Christians hope to experience the blessings of prayer more fully? Can their prayers ever become more like what God wants them to be? What's the problem with prayer? In the chapters that follow, we will look for answers to these questions, answers that will equip Christians to enjoy more completely the many riches of prayer.

Where do we go for help? Because God's Word is our guide in all matters of faith and life, we look in the Bible for solutions to our problems with prayer. Immediately our hearts turn to the Lord's Prayer or a few other passages in the New Testament, but the Bible has much more to say about prayer than this. The Old Testament Psalms, for example, contain more prayers than any other portion of Scripture. They comprise a collection of inspired prayers that God's people sang and recited in all kinds of circumstances: during worship, while traveling along the road, and in the daily activities of life at home. They project the full range of human emotions, from exuberant joy to frantic despair. Sadly, believers often ignore the Psalms and many other passages in which the Bible teaches us how to pray. In this study, however, we will not limit ourselves to a few well-known passages. We will take a close look at the Psalms and other less familiar portions of the Bible and find many new insights into this area of our lives.

Before going further, we must stop and carefully define what we are talking about. The word "prayer" can refer to many things. A child's poem of thanks before dinner, passing thoughts directed toward God, deeply felt laments, and joyous praises are commonly identified as prayer. Occasionally, the meaning of the term is stretched to include other sorts of activities—a painting, a musical recital, or a liturgical dance. Most people will agree, however, that these are extraordinary uses of the word.

From a biblical point of view, prayer may be defined as *a believer's communication with God*. This definition suggests three main elements in prayer: (1) *God*, (2) *the believer*, and (3) *the communication*. If one of these components is missing, prayer cannot occur. A quiet church building may not be accessible; we may not have much time;

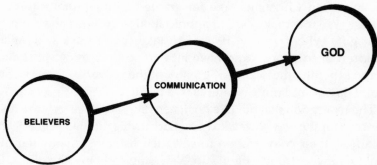

Fig. 1.1. The Elements of Prayer

friends and prayer partners may not be around. But as good and helpful as these elements may be, none is essential to prayer. Take away God, the believer, or the communication, however, and prayer becomes impossible. Without God no one listens; without the believer no one speaks; without communication nothing is said (see fig. 1.1).

These three elements are essential for fruitful and fulfilling communication with God. Ignoring any one of them paralyzes prayer, but attending to them all will move us toward a more vibrant prayer life.

The Recipient of Prayer

According to our definition, the first element of prayer is God. Every Christian at one time or another wonders exactly what role God plays in prayer. Scripture teaches that God has many roles. For example, as the Lord and giver of life, God sustains us, making it possible for us to pray. More than this, He forgives sin that would otherwise prevent us from approaching Him. Perhaps His most significant role, however, is that He receives our prayers. As the psalmist wrote,

Hear my prayer, *O God;*
 listen to the words of my mouth (Ps. 54:2).*

*All Scripture quotations are from the Holy Bible, New International Version, © 1973, 1978, 1984 by the International Bible Society. Italics indicate emphasis added.

All too often Christians take for granted God's promise to hear prayer. We must take care to appreciate this gracious and remarkable gift. When we find it hard to take time to talk with small children or to people who have little to offer us, how we should marvel that the transcendent Creator of the universe stoops low to hear His frail and finite creatures. We talk to God and He listens.

The realization that our Creator listens should shock us into a new concern for the way we talk to Him. Early in life, human beings learn to adjust their conversation to suit their listeners. Soon after my family moved from Virginia to New England, my five-year-old daughter began speaking English in two distinct ways. With her mother and me, she spoke with the slight southern accent characteristic of our home in Virginia. With her neighborhood friends, however, she talked as if she had lived all her life in the suburbs of Boston. Adults make similar adjustments in their conversations. Husbands and wives converse in ways they would never talk with others. Employees speak to each other differently than they talk to their employer. Our ordinary conversations reflect our attitudes toward the listener, and the same is true in prayer. Our thoughts and attitudes about God largely determine how we speak to Him.

Notice the prayers of someone from a church background different from your own. Believers who think of God primarily as a close personal friend will offer prayers that are very casual and informal. But if they think of God as the sovereign King of the universe, their prayers will tend to be more formal and reverent. Christians adjust their communication with God to match their perception of Him.

Our concept of God affects every aspect of our prayer life. Many Christians, for instance, are bored with prayer largely because their perception of God is so narrow. It is no wonder that we lose interest in prayer when we severely limit our conception of God. By emphasizing one or two of God's characteristics to the near exclusion of all the others, we unwittingly reduce Him to a two-dimensional, black-and-white picture. Imagine talking to a black-and-white sketch of a dear friend. Such a monologue would surely be monotonous and unrewarding. Sadly, prayer can become boring for the same reason. If we do not deepen our awareness of God and His many characteristics, our prayers will fall short of their full potential.

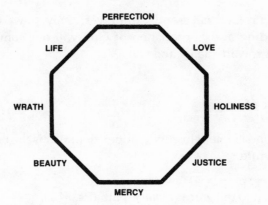

Fig. 1.2. The Wonder of God

The Bible describes God as mysteriously and wonderfully multi-faceted. He is love, holiness, justice, mercy, beauty, perfection, life, wrath—to name only a few of His characteristics. All of God's attributes reveal different aspects of His personality. Depending on our circumstances, different dimensions of His character will mean more to us than others. Yet, at no time should the Christian be satisfied with a one-sided conception of God. For our prayers to be filled with life and vitality, we must always strive to deepen our awareness of God in all the ways He is revealed in Scripture (see fig. 1.2).

The Psalms illustrate the importance of focusing on the many sides of God's character. In their prayers, the psalmists mention many attributes of God. His reliability is the focus of one prayer:

> To you I call, O LORD my Rock;
>   do not turn a deaf ear to me (Ps. 28:1).

Another psalm emphasizes His strength:

> I love you, O LORD, my strength (Ps. 18:1).

Like the psalmists, we should learn to focus on the wondrous qualities of God as we pray. If we are hurting, we may look upon God's love and thereby experience the easing of our pain. If we are reeling from wrongs done to us, we may focus on God's justice.

A focus on God is essential to prayer. Only as we deepen our understanding and appreciation of God will our communication with Him grow in quality and value.

The Source of Prayer

The second element in our definition of prayer is the believer. The psalmist wrote,

> Hear *my* prayer, O God;
>   listen to the words of *my* mouth (Ps. 54:2).

Prayer always involves a human source. God Himself ultimately gives us the ability to pray, but the human instrument still serves as the creaturely source of communication. Prayer emerges from the human mind and heart. Even when Christians use words already written or passed down by others, they adopt them as their own when they offer them to God. In this sense, we are the source of communication with God.

Because prayer finds its source in believers, we also should pay attention to ourselves as we pray. The more aware we are of ourselves, the more sincere our prayers will become. I once participated in a communication workshop for married couples. One of the most memorable lessons I learned was how to "speak for myself." In the group we discovered how frequently we fail to examine our own thoughts and feelings as we talk with our spouses. We concentrate on everything except clearly expressing what is deep within us. How little we know about ourselves and how poorly we express what we do know! Self-understanding and self-expression are fundamental to all fruitful communication. Communication with God is no different. We must learn how to "speak for ourselves" when we pray.

The psalmists are deeply aware of their own thoughts and attitudes in prayer. At times they express jubilation:

> Praise the LORD.
> Praise the LORD, O my soul (Ps. 146:1).

WHAT ARE MY
ATTITUDES, IDEAS,
CIRCUMSTANCES?

Fig. 1.3. Self-Awareness in Prayer

Sometimes they present strong desires:

> All my longings lie open before you, O Lord;
>   my sighing is not hidden from you.
> My heart pounds, my strength fails me;
>   even the light has gone from my eyes (Ps. 38:9-10).

At other times, they even admit to deep discouragement:

> My God, my God, why have you forsaken me?
>   Why are you so far from saving me,
>   so far from the words of my groaning?
> O my God, I cry out by day, but you do not answer,
>   by night, and am not silent (Ps. 22:1-2).

These examples illustrate how self-awareness can add a profound dimension to prayer. We must thoroughly assess what is going on within us: How do I feel? What am I thinking? What are my attitudes, ideas, and circumstances? (see fig. 1.3).

People involve themselves to varying degrees in their daily conversations. At times superficial responses will suffice—"How are you?" "Just fine!" We make these exchanges out of polite custom with little concern for sincerity. But at other times when we sense the magnitude of a situation, we feel the need to search inside ourselves and to express our more profound feelings. Who can be satisfied with cliches when a healthy baby is born to close friends? Who can hide behind polite superficiality when a broken marriage is healed? Young men and women get to know each other only after they begin to talk frankly about themselves and their feelings. At times, even words of anger can deepen a relationship. Superficial conversation will suffice for some situations, but weighty and personal matters require words that stem from the heart.

Do our prayers arise from our hearts? Often Christians utter one trite phrase after another when praying. They mimic prayers they have heard even if they do not express their own thoughts or feelings. In fact, many Christians would be shocked to hear a prayer expressing attitudes of sorrow and severe disappointment. Instead, we expect a series of pious phrases that will get us safely through the ritual. Unfortunately, we often get just what we want—a mere ritual. If Christians want to establish deep, personal contact with God, they must forsake superficial prayer. Like the psalmists, we must examine and express ourselves as honestly and completely as possible.

The Words of Communication

Communication is the third element essential to prayer. Christians must also be conscious of their words when they pray. The psalmist makes this clear:

> Hear my *prayer*, O God;
>   listen to the *words of my mouth* (Ps. 54:2).

No doubt, words are unable to express all that is in our hearts. But at such times we can take comfort in knowing that the Spirit understands us and intercedes on our behalf:

> In the same way, the Spirit helps us in our weakness. We do not know what we ought to pray, but the Spirit himself intercedes for us with groans that words cannot express. And he who searches our hearts knows the mind of the Spirit, because the Spirit intercedes for the saints in accordance with God's will (Rom. 8:26-27).

Despite the Spirit's work, however, we should be very concerned with our words—words that will either hinder or enhance our communication with God.

A funeral is no place to crack a joke. A library is not the place to shout a football cheer. To entertain, we may tell a story. To get information, we may ask a question. Unfortunately, however, Christians seldom use that much variety when they talk with God. They tend to follow one or two patterns for prayer no matter what their circumstances or intentions may be. Though one Christian's prayers may differ somewhat from another's, they generally follow similar patterns. Some believers use the design "Jesus, Others, Yourself" (JOY). Others follow the pattern "Adoration, Confession, Thanksgiving, Supplication" (ACTS). These models help many Christians, especially new believers, to balance the various parts of prayer. Yet, all models are limited in their ability to meet the diverse needs we experience. Even the Lord's Prayer is not to be used as a strict model for communication with God in all situations (Matt. 6:9-13; Luke 11:2-4). Although it is a rich resource for learning how to pray, the Lord's Prayer is only a summary outline, which Jesus gave as a general guide to prayer, not a specific rule. Jesus Himself prayed in ways that did not follow precisely the model of the Lord's Prayer (cf. John 17:1-26). No single model is able to communicate adequately all the concerns of the human heart.

For this reason, the Psalms serve well as examples of prayer. The psalmists lift up praises:

> Give thanks to the LORD, for he is good.
>> His love endures forever (Ps. 136:1).

They offer laments:

> We are consumed by your anger
>> and terrified by your indignation (Ps. 90:7).

They express statements:

> Then will I go to the altar of God,
>> to God, my joy and my delight.
> I will praise you with the harp,
>> O God, my God (Ps. 43:4).

And they ask questions:

> Will the Lord reject us forever?
> Will he never show his favor again? (Ps. 77:7).

MANY DIFFERENT THINGS
TO SAY IN PRAYER

Fig. 1.4. Variation of Communication in Prayer

The psalmists used all kinds of expressions and patterns in prayer. And so should modern believers. A mother who has just seen her stillborn child may be unable to begin her prayer with adoration. She is free to express her grief and pain. A father does not have to confess his sins before giving thanks for the accomplishments of his children. He may simply praise God. Following the example of the psalmists, Christians should vary the content and form of their prayers according to their circumstances and their responses to them (see fig. 1.4).

Variety in prayer is vital to effective communication with God. I remember taking a long bus trip as a teen-ager and being assigned to sit with someone I did not know very well. Being separated from my friends was bad enough, but my partner made the trip almost unbearable. All she could talk about were her good grades in school. Every time I tried to change the topic, she returned to this same theme. Needless to say, I was miserable. Following the same patterns again and again will destroy a prayer life, just as surely as it destroys earthly conversation. The same words, said in the same way, at the same time, over and over will drain all the life out of communication with God. Yet, if we learn from the psalmists and other biblical figures and begin to imitate the freedom and creativity of their prayers, then we can expect our communication with God to grow richer and more inspiring by the day.

The chapters that follow will look carefully at the three crucial elements of prayer outlined in this chapter. By closely examining what the Bible says about God, ourselves, and our communication, we can begin to overcome our frustrating problems with prayer and experience more fully the rich blessings of talking with God.

Review Questions

1. What is the definition of prayer given in this chapter? What is the biblical support for this definition? Distinguish between the essential and nonessential aspects of prayer.

2. Why may we say that God is the recipient of prayer? How can God's listening role influence the way we pray? Why do we continually need to deepen and clarify our concept of God?

3. What role does the believer play in prayer? Why should believers pay attention to themselves in prayer? Can we pay too much attention to ourselves?

4. What role do our words play in prayer? Why are they important? Why do we need variety in the way we say our prayers?

Exercises

1. Carefully read Psalm 56:1-13. (a) List three ways the psalmist thinks about God. (b) Also note three ways he shows awareness of himself in prayer. (c) Finally, list three ways in which this prayer differs from your usual pattern of prayer.

2. Read the following prayers. Compare and contrast the attention paid to God, the focus on the believer, and the styles of communication.

    O YOU who have ordered this wondrous world, fill my heart with trust in You at all times. May I commit myself to Your never-ending purposes for this life and the life to come. Amen.

    O LORD of all purity and goodness, we pray that You will

purify our lives. Help us each day to know more of You, and use us to show Yourself to others. Make us humble and loving; make us ready for service. We ask not only that You will keep us safe, but also that You will keep us ever loyal. Amen.

3. Using the form below as much as possible, write out a prayer in which you commit yourself to focusing attention on God, yourself, and your communication. Be sure to mention why you hope to do this. Then read this prayer before the Lord.

O Lord, as we begin this study of prayer, we seek Your grace.

Help us to focus our hearts on You because _____
                                              (Express your reason for this request.)

_____

_____ .

Help us to look carefully at ourselves because _____

_____
                        (Express your reason for this request.)

_____ .

Also help us to give attention to what we say because _____

_____
                        (Express your reason for this request.)

_____ .

As You bless us in this endeavor, we will _____
                                          (Make a promise to God.)

_____

_____ . Amen.

Extended Exercise

Before three meals this week, take a few moments to write down a four- or five-sentence blessing for the meal. Be sure to vary your focus on God, yourself, and the kind of prayer you are offering. Keep these prayers and compare them through the week. Ask yourself, "How am I deepening my awareness of God, myself, and my prayers?"

Part One

LOOKING AT
GOD

Father, God. Thank you for this meal.
I pray that you bless our body through
this meal. Please bless our family time
together through the meal we are about to
eat. Please bring joy and happiness to this
Table. Help us to understand you joy in our
heart by communicating with each other
during this meal

2

A Servant's Gaze

Thy grace, O Father, give,
I humbly thee implore;
And let thy mercy bless
Thy servant more and more.
        Gregory Nazianzen
        325-90

People look at each other in many different ways. A lawyer's penetrating stare at a witness differs greatly from the longing gaze of two people in love. A doctor's impersonal examination of a patient hardly compares with a mother's tender attention to her own sick child. Beyond this, the way we look at other people changes from moment to moment. A grandmother's fond gaze can change dramatically when she sees her two-year-old grandchild wobbling toward her favorite crystal vase. A friend's thoughtless remark may turn a smile into a resentful grimace.

Just as in human relationships, believers look at God in a variety of ways. At times we look with eyes of intimacy and love; at other times awe and reverence fill our hearts. In the previous chapter we discovered that giving God our attention is vital to prayer. But what kind of attention should we give Him? What attitude should our look reflect? Scripture sets many options before us, but fundamental to them all is the ability to look at God with a servant's gaze.

Dependence on God

When we consider how dependent we are on God, we under-stand that Christians should take on the attitude of a needy servant. Most Christians acknowledge their dependence on God in some way but easily forget the extent of this need. The psalmists speak clearly about the range of human dependence. Psalm 104, for instance, describes God's construction of the universe:

> He wraps himself in light as with a garment;
> he stretches out the heavens like a tent
> and lays the beams of his upper chambers on their waters.
> He set the earth on its foundations;
> it can never be moved (vv. 2-3a, 5).

In light of God's magnificent power, the psalmist also speaks of the various creatures of the earth:

> These all look to you
> to give them their food at the proper time.
> When you give it to them,
> they gather it up;
> when you open your hand,
> they are satisfied with good things.
> When you hide your face,
> they are terrified;
> when you take away their breath,
> they die and return to the dust (vv. 27-29).

God's sustaining hand extends to all the dimensions of the universe. If He were to remove His care, all would return to nothing. Paul summarizes this truth by saying,

> He is before all things, and in him all
> things hold together (Col. 1:17).

All aspects of creation—great and small, animate and inanimate—constantly depend on God's sustaining power. No aspect of the universe is beyond His care; no part of creation exists independent of Him (see fig. 2.1).

Recognizing our extensive need for God helps us determine how

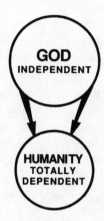

Fig. 2.1. Our Dependence on God

to look at Him as we pray. In Psalm 123:2 we read,

> As the eyes of slaves look to the hand of their master,
>   as the eyes of a maid look to the hand of her mistress,
> so our eyes look to the LORD our God,
>   till he shows us his mercy.

This passage likens the communion of prayer to the relationship of a servant and master. Today, this image conjures up visions of terrible racial and social abuse. In the Old Testament world, however, servants and masters were not always at odds. In fact, wealthier Israelites could show great kindness to their destitute neighbors by hiring them as servants. In such cases, only the master's generosity stood between a servant and starvation. As servants of God, we are in utter need of His provision. His hand alone comes between us and eternal death. And for this we owe Him our servitude. We can think of God in many ways: a loving father, a powerful king, a righteous judge, to mention only a few. Yet fundamental to all of these perspectives is the view of ourselves as needy servants. Only when we acknowledge our complete dependence can we begin to enter prayer with a proper focus on God.

Our status as needy servants reveals the importance of taking time to pray. Many Christians complain of being too busy to talk with God. We are always on the run—working overtime, taking the children here and there, preparing for school, going to church, and entertaining family and friends. Unhappily, we begin to live as if we do not need God at all. Many people eventually see the futility of this way of life. They watch their best efforts eroded by causes beyond their control. Men and women work hard to reach the top of their professions, only to learn that they are dying of incurable diseases. Parents strive for years to raise their children, only to see them rebel against their training. After going through such trage- dies, many Christians finally realize they need God and resolve to take time for prayer. Unfortunately, this realization often comes only after great suffering.

I once spoke with an older woman reputed to be a prayer warrior. Church members frequently asked her to pray for their special needs. When I questioned this woman about her devotion to prayer, she told me this story with tears in her eyes. Early in her adult life she was widowed and left with a son. She devoted herself to making this son the finest Christian man possible. She read books on rearing children; she sent him to the best schools; she spent great quantities of time with him. "But," she confessed, "I hardly ever prayed for him." Her story had a tragic ending. Beset with one failure after another, her twenty-five-year-old son committed suicide. "Only then," she said, "did I see that I had depended too much on myself and not enough on God." So today she devotes herself to prayer. She turns from creaturely impotence to the omnipotent Creator. Tragic experiences like this demonstrate the importance of relying on God and not on our own feeble strength. He is our Sovereign; our destinies lie in His hands. For this reason, looking to God in prayer is an essential part of the Christian life.

Understanding our dependence on God also prevents us from praying simply out of religious obligation. Christian leaders often try to motivate others to pray by speaking of prayer as a necessary act of obedience. To be sure, prayer is a Christian duty. Paul com- manded us to "pray continually" (I Thess. 5:17). However, over- emphasizing the obligatory character of prayer can actually cause Christians to pray less.

This principle shows itself in human relations. We see an old friend during the holiday season and promise to write throughout the year. Before we know it, several months have passed and we still have not written. The longer we wait the greater the difficulty in writing. After a year passes, we virtually cannot pick up the pen. Similarly, when we view prayer primarily as a duty, our failure to pray leads to guilt. This guilt, in turn, makes talking with God even more difficult.

To avoid this downward spiral, we should stop viewing prayer solely as an obligation and see it also as essential for life. Every kind of prayer ultimately rests upon our dependence on God. Petitions are based on what we need. The confession of sin points to our hope for forgiveness from God. Intercession expresses the needs of others. Praise recognizes that God blesses us with great gifts. If we fully consider our absolute dependence on God, prayer becomes more than an obligation; it becomes a way to acknowledge the one who provides for all our needs.

Given this perspective, we can remove prayer from our list of boring chores and begin to rank it where it belongs—among the essentials for meaningful existence. Fruitful, life-giving prayer rests firmly on the foundation of recognizing our need for God; it begins with the attitude of a dependent servant.

An Intense Gaze

One of the first public speeches I ever delivered was in a junior high classroom. For many days I gathered the pertinent information—what, where, how, why. I prepared an outline and practiced dramatic techniques to enhance my presentation. I rehearsed until I was certain of a good grade. When the big day arrived, I gave my talk precisely as I had prepared it. Much to my dismay, however, the teacher was not as pleased as I. Her comment was stinging. "Fine content, but you never looked at us. I wasn't sure whether you were more interested in us or your notes." That day I learned an important lesson. We show our regard for others by looking at them when we talk.

Psalm 123:2 suggests that the same is true when we talk to God. A servant's look is not an occasional glance at God but an intense gaze at Him:

As the eyes of slaves look to the hand of their master,
    as the eyes of a maid look to the hand of her mistress,

so our eyes look to the LORD our God,
  till he shows us his mercy.

These servants fix their eyes on the Master's hand. Their attention is so intense that they refuse to turn away "till he shows us his mercy." No daydreaming hampers this kind of prayer. The look of a servant is an intense focus on the Master.

This portrait stands in sharp contrast to many of our prayers. Instead of centering on God, most Christians only glance occasionally in His direction. Ordinarily our prayers begin with an address toward God: "Our Father," "Lord Jesus," "Heavenly Father." We also tend to intersperse His name throughout a prayer: "Lord, . . . Lord, . . . Lord, . . ." Typically, our prayers also close with "in Jesus' name, Amen." In the majority of cases, however, this is nearly all the attention God receives. In a prayer lasting ten minutes, we will usually spend less than sixty seconds focusing primarily on God. Apart from a few phrases now and then, we could as easily be wishing on a star as praying to God.

This neglect of God reveals a basic misunderstanding about prayer. We often treat prayer like a spiritual shopping list. We walk into God's general store, give a perfunctory nod in His direction, and then proceed to the real reason we came—the grocery list. We spend the bulk of our time listing one request after another, and God Himself takes second place. In fact, this habit of ignoring God suggests that we would prefer to find Him absent from the store so we would not have to bother with Him at all. How easy it is to forget that we are dealing with a divine Person, not a heavenly mail-order catalog. When we focus too much on *what* we need, we are bound to neglect the One *whom* we need (see fig. 2.2).

These observations should make each of us stop and examine our prayers. What do we think about as we pray? Christians can easily become so absorbed with their material and spiritual needs that they crowd out all thoughts of God. When a friend is seriously ill, it is normal to dwell on that friend. When facing troubling circumstances, we are naturally preoccupied with them. We must pay attention to these things to some degree. Nevertheless, even in extreme situations like these we must guard against reducing prayer solely to concern for our needs. Sporadic and halfhearted attention to God

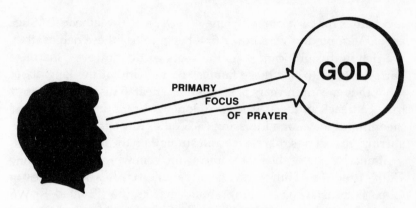

Fig. 2.2. A Servant's Intense Gaze

will never yield life-enriching prayer. We must cultivate the look of a servant, an intense gaze at God.

Looking and Addressing

We can develop an intense gaze toward God in many ways. To some extent, each person has to go about this task in his or her own way. Not every suggestion offered in these chapters will be suitable for every person. Yet, many biblical principles offer valuable guidance for us all. In the remainder of this chapter we will explore one way to begin giving God more attention in prayer.

One helpful method for focusing on God is to address Him meaningfully. Usually we address God by only a few titles: "Father," "God," "Lord," "Jesus," or "Christ." All of these names are full of wonderful meaning and should be used in prayer. Yet, very often Christians adopt these particular terms so much that they lose their significance. How many times do we stop and think about what it means to call out, "Father," "God," "Lord," "Jesus," or "Christ"? For all the attention we usually give to these words, we may just as easily say, "Hey, You up there!" The habit of addressing God in these familiar ways can cause our minds to drift away from intense concern with Him.

Husbands and wives frequently develop endearing names and

nicknames for each other: "Honey," "Dear," "Sweetheart," "Sugar." Undoubtedly, when they first begin to use these names, they are rich with significance. As the years go by, however, marriage partners tend to use these familiar terms without thinking about what they meant in years past. Even in a heated disagreement they may call each other "Dear" or "Honey." Searching for new and meaningful ways of addressing each other can refresh a marriage, stirring up feelings that revive and strengthen the relationship.

Similarly, one of the first steps toward renewing our attention to God is to address Him with variety. Variation creates new interest in God. For instance, thinking about Him as the "Exalted King," "Master of the Universe," "Giver of Life," or "Mighty Fortress" immediately stirs our hearts. Unusual ways of calling on God evoke all sorts of concepts and attitudes. They help us focus more clearly on who God is and what He does for us.

The Bible provides countless ways of addressing God. Consider, for instance, the many titles given to Jesus in the Old and New Testaments: "righteous Judge" (2 Tim. 4:8), "Head of the Church" (cf. Eph. 1:22), "Firstborn of creation" (cf. Col. 1:15), "firstborn among many brothers" (Rom. 8:29), "King of Kings" (Rev. 19:16), "Morning Star" (Rev. 22:16), "Advocate" (cf. 1 John 2:1), "Word of life" (1 John 1:1), "Alpha and Omega" (cf. Rev. 1:8), "chief cornerstone" (Eph. 2:20), "Prince of Peace" (Isa. 9:6), "Lamb of God" (John 1:29), "Resurrection and Life" (cf. John 11:25). Sadly, we seldom hear these titles of Christ used in prayer. Yet, each of them is packed full of powerful significance that draws us toward Him. (See appendix A for a fuller list of divine names and titles.)

Recently, one of my students determined to address God in unusual ways while praying before his church. The church members responded with enthusiasm. They reported that his choice of words caught their attention and involved them with God more than ever before. More fully utilizing the varied ways we may address God often brings an astounding awakening of interest and devotion (see fig. 2.3).

If so many possibilities for addressing God are available to us, how should we choose from among them? Psalm 68:5 illustrates a useful principle:

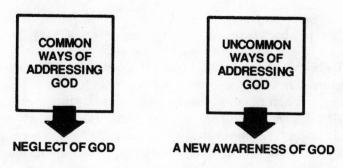

Fig. 2.3. Addressing God in New Ways

A father to the fatherless, a defender of widows,
  is God in his holy dwelling.

This passage expresses the truth that different people need God in different ways. God reveals Himself as a protecting husband to the widow and as a father to the orphan. His character is so rich and multifaceted that He deals with us according to our individual needs. Jesus demonstrated this divine quality in His own life. To the sick, He was the Healer. To those in darkness, He was the Light of the World. To the struggling and oppressed, He came as liberating King. The gospel presents Jesus as one who meets the variety of needs created by sin and rebellion against God. In His grace, God reveals Himself as the answer to our individual circumstances.

In the Psalms, God is frequently addressed in ways that correspond directly to the needs of the one praying. When the psalmist desires forgiveness, he addresses God appropriately:

Restore us again, *O God our Savior,*
  and put away your displeasure toward us (Ps. 85:4).

In a context dealing with the reversal of calamity, the psalmist says,

Lord, you have been *our dwelling place*
  throughout all generations (Ps. 90:1).

When retribution for wickedness is in view, the psalmist addresses God by these words:

Rise up, *O Judge of the earth;*
   pay back to the proud what they deserve (Ps. 94:2).

Today, we too may call on God in ways that are appropriate to our concerns. In times of sorrow, we may refer to Him as our "Comforter." When discouraged, we may address Him as our "Hope" and "Courage." Joyful prayers may speak of God as our "Strength" and "Song." Whatever the case, addressing God in ways that are particularly relevant to the rest of our prayer enlivens our attention to Him. In this way, we avoid focusing simply on our needs and move closer to centering our prayers on God Himself, the One who can deal with our needs.

In this chapter, we have seen several important aspects of a prayerful focus on God. Basic to all prayer is the attitude of a needy servant. Our hearts must be intensely centered on God as we pray. This intense gaze may be enhanced by using variety and selectivity when addressing God. With these ideas in mind, we can make our prayers a servant's gaze.

Review Questions

1. How much do we depend on God? How is this concept basic to prayer?

2. Why should prayer be an intense gaze at God? How do Christians often give very little attention to God when they pray?

3. What are some of the many ways in which the Bible addresses God? What are the values and dangers of addressing God with commonly used names and titles? What principle of selection should be used when addressing God in prayer?

Exercises

1. List four areas in your life in which you find it easy to forget how much you need God's help. Describe why you need God in these areas.

2. Match the following addresses of God with an appropriate request. Why did you choose those particular matches?

Address		Request	
7	Light of the World	1	let us take refuge in You
9	Fountain of Wisdom	2	mold us into the image of Christ
5	Lord of Heavenly Armies	3	keep us hidden from harm
2	Master Potter	4	assist us in this task
3	Safe Hiding Place	5	strike down our enemies
4	Helper	6	bring an end to war
1	Rock and Fortress	7	break forth into our darkness
10	Bread of Life	8	give us the powers we need
6	Prince of Peace	9	grant us insight
8	Giver of Gifts	10	fill our hungry souls
11	Almighty Sovereign	11	display Your power

3. Write a six-to-eight-sentence prayer in which you tell God several ways in which you need Him. Use the form below as much as possible. (Also see appendix A.)

How we need You, _Our Powerfull Helper_
(Address God in a particular way.)

_____ .

When we think about our dependence on You, we bow in humility and gratitude. We depend on you to be _Our master_

_____
(Describe a quality of God that meets some of your needs.)

_____

because _You are master Potter, Wisdom giver, greatest_
(Describe how you need God.)
Provider, Prince of Peace, greatest Phisician,
Father of Fatherless, My hope & Courage,
Judge of The earth & bread of life .

We confess O Lord that we often forget how much we depend on You. How wonderfully You provide for our needs. Amen.

Extended Exercise

Take the time this week to pray at least three times without asking
for anything. Instead, use the time of prayer only to reflect carefully
on your need for a number of the qualities of God. Try to focus on a
different characteristic of God each time. You may find the form in
exercise 3 helpful.

3

Fascination With God's Character

When was the last time you were fascinated with God? At one time or another, all of us have met someone we greatly admire. We admire athletes for their strength and musicians for their talents. The abilities of the sculptor amaze us. The charisma of the statesman fascinates us. Yet, we are seldom so amazed or fascinated with God. The Christian life is full of opportunities to experience a sense of wonder and amazement with God. These opportunities come in many Christian activities, but one of the most important opportunities is prayer. In this chapter, we will explore some of the ways in which prayer can nurture a fascination with God.

Contemplating God's Character

Fascination with God results from enthusiastic appreciation for Him. Although unbelievers are blind to the wonder of God, believers are given precious glimpses into God's glory. In fact, the more we concentrate on discovering God's incomparable qualities,

27

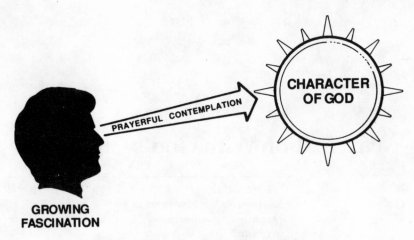

GROWING
FASCINATION

Fig. 3.1. Fascination Through Contemplation

the more awestruck we become. Consider the wonder of God—His
beauty is contemplated by one psalmist:

> One thing I ask of the LORD,
>   this is what I seek:
> that I may dwell in the house of the LORD
>   all the days of my life,
> to gaze upon the beauty of the LORD
>   and to seek him in his temple (Ps. 27:4).

His justice is the focus of another psalm:

> Righteousness and justice are the foundation of your throne;
> Love and faithfulness go before you (Ps. 89:14).

These words express an attitude of wonder and amazement. The
magnitude and perfection of God's character overwhelm our feeble
earthbound minds. How can anyone be so perfect? Who can even
begin to compare with God in His magnificence?

Regrettably, many Christians go for long periods of time without
this sense of fascination. God becomes such an ordinary part of their
lives that their thoughts about Him become bland and uninspiring.

In many areas of life, familiarity stifles the ability to appreciate and
admire another person. When a couple first meet and marry, their

affection is strong. A few years and a couple of children later, that colorful, warm relationship can diminish into a cold gray. Familiarity transforms that paragon of masculinity and that model of femininity into fixtures of everyday life.

In the same way, believers find their love for God fading. As Jesus warned the church at Ephesus,

> I hold this against you: You have forsaken
> your first love (Rev. 2:4).

Like the shine of a new car, our amazement with God may dull with time. We become so accustomed to His care that we lose our appreciation for Him. Just as we need to polish and shine a car again and again, we must also work at keeping our awareness of God bright and radiant. We must continually search for ways to rediscover His wonder.

Prayer is an excellent means of refreshing our appreciation for God. Simply telling God about His excellent qualities stirs our hearts to wonder. In everyday life, we think a lot about the people we admire. We sit and daydream about them; we talk to our friends about them. The more we talk, the more we admire them.

A friend once invited me to attend a special university lecture. I was not very excited about staying late because the lecturer was not familiar to me. But as a courtesy to my friend, I stayed—even though I was certain it would be boring. As I listened to a professor introduce the lecturer and heard compliment upon compliment lavished on this man, I found my attitude changing. By the end of the introduction I was eager to hear his speech. Hearing about this man filled me with admiration for him. In a similar way, through prayer we have the privilege of reviewing God's qualities. As we contemplate the wonder of God's character, fascination for Him will grow and grow (see fig. 3.1).

Psalm 18:1-3 shows clearly how fascination and contemplation are tied together in prayer:

> I love you, O LORD, my strength.

> The LORD is my rock, my fortress and my deliverer;
>   My God is my rock, in whom I take refuge.
> He is my shield and the horn of my salvation,
>   my stronghold.

I call to the LORD, who is worthy of praise,
and I am saved from my enemies.

The psalmist is delighted with God. Psalm 18 is a thanksgiving expressing gratitude for a blessing from God. God's work on his behalf causes the psalmist to raise his voice in unabashed enthusiasm. He exclaims, "I love you, O LORD!" (18:1). Yet, how does this loving appreciation show itself? The psalmist focuses on God's character. In his opening verses, he piles up metaphors and descriptions in his effort to express God's goodness. He calls out, "LORD," "my rock," "my fortress," "my deliverer," "my God," "my shield," "horn of my salvation," "my stronghold," and the One "who is worthy of praise." These multiple descriptions illustrate the psalmist's enthusiastic attention to God in his prayer. His admiration for God leads him to talk about His character.

Regrettably, Christians typically ignore the qualities of God in their prayers. They may say something like, "Thank You for who You are," but they never stop to talk much about just who God is. Deep reflection on God's character is not necessary for all prayers. But if our prayers regularly exclude reflection on God's magnificent qualities, we will miss the joy of discovering afresh the wonder of God. (See appendix B for a list of divine attributes.)

Contemplating Through Description

Contemplation of God's character can take many forms. Biblical prayers often do this by including brief descriptions of His attributes. When we describe God, His attributes become more central to our thoughts and influence us on many levels. By speaking of His mercy, we feel His kindness and patience with our shortcomings. By reflecting on His intimate love, we experience His warmth and gentle embrace. These and other dimensions of God's character can be described in prayer so that we are moved to ever-deeper appreciation of Him.

Many biblical prayers contain brief descriptions of God. The psalmists frequently are not satisfied to address God by a simple name or title. For instance, in Psalm 65:2 we read,

O you who hear prayer,
    to you all men will come.

Again in Psalm 68:35 we find,

You are awesome, O God, in your sanctuary;
    the God of Israel gives power and strength to his people.

Praise be to God!

In both of these prayers the psalmist describes particular aspects of God's character. Solomon's prayer at the dedication of the temple is particularly graphic:

O LORD, God of Israel, there is no God like you in heaven above or on earth below—you who keep your covenant of love with your servants who continue wholeheartedly in your way (1 Kings 8:23).

We find another outstanding example in Daniel's well-known prayer:

O Lord, the great and awesome God, who keeps his covenant of love with all who love him and obey his commands (Dan. 9:4).

These two examples demonstrate how elaborate prayerful sketches of God can be. Jesus Himself used this method of focusing on God. He wanted His followers to remember the sovereignty of their divine Father, so He taught them to pray,

Our father *in heaven* (Matt 6:9).

Put simply, the practice of including descriptions of God in our prayers helps us focus more intensely on the character of God. To be sure, talking about God's qualities does not guarantee a deeper appreciation for Him. We can pass over these words as thoughtlessly as we can His many names and titles. Even so, contemplation of His attributes provides an opportunity for a fresh look at God. In the midst of prayer, briefly recounting one of God's outstanding attributes can move us to exchange the thoughts of this world for the contemplation of God's glory.

Descriptions of God are particularly significant when they are matched with the broader concerns of a prayer. In the case of Daniel 9:4-19, Daniel prays that God will return the Jewish captives to their land. In line with this intense concern, Daniel opens his prayer with several descriptions of God. He speaks of God as "great and awesome" (9:4). Daniel hopes to see Babylon's power over Israel broken. So he focuses on the majesty of God. He also speaks of God as the one who "keeps his covenant of love with all who love Him and obey His commands" (9:4). Since he hopes that God will continue to be faithful to promises He has made, Daniel concentrates on His faithfulness as well. By contemplating these divine characteristics in his prayer, Daniel finds the assurance he needs.

We, too, face circumstances that turn our hearts toward God in particular ways. Describing Him in ways that answer our needs brings us hope and strength. I once counseled a young man who suffered from a terribly low self-image stemming in part from guilt over events in his past. After praying with him several times, I began to notice that he always emphasized the lofty, powerful, and fearful character of God. Justice and judgment were his constant themes. No wonder he could not find a sense of forgiveness. He never dwelt upon the mercy, patience, and kindness of God. When an opportunity presented itself, I suggested that he pray contemplating God's forgiveness and patience. After he tried it, he still had not completely resolved his problems, but the look on his face told me that he had begun to see the importance of focusing on this side of God as well. At times we need to be assured of God's love. At other times, we need to remember His judgment. Whatever our circumstances, prayerful descriptions of God become a gateway into the renewal of faith (see fig. 3.2).

Contemplating Through Metaphors

Metaphors are also a great help in contemplating God's character. A metaphor is a form of description in which one thing is compared with another. "He is an ox," implies that the man is big and strong. "She is a gem," implies that the woman is precious and beautiful. Precisely speaking, metaphors are implicit comparisons that are

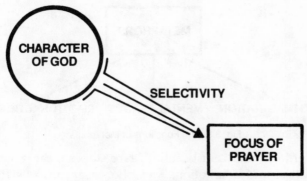

Fig. 3.2. Selective Descriptions

made without the words *like* or *as*. However, we will use the term more broadly to include comparisons in general. We have already seen the value of describing God as we pray. Now we will look into the importance of using metaphors in speaking of God.

Why do we use metaphors? Why not simply describe things in plain language? A person may choose to use a metaphor for many reasons. We will look at only three.

First, metaphors require our imaginations to determine precise meanings. "He is a real bear," could imply that the person is big and burly or that he is grouchy. We must think about the comparison and decide. Metaphors invite the mind to consider the many ways in which one thing is like another. In this manner, they cause an inquiring person to think more deeply and imaginatively about the things being compared.

Second, metaphors create vivid mental images. As we consider a metaphor, many different sights, sounds, tastes, smells, and textures come to mind. Contemplating the comparison of a man with an ox inevitably brings to mind a mental image of the animal. We can see its broad shoulders and hear it strain under a heavy load. The comparison of a woman with a gem evokes images of valuable stones reflecting a spectrum of brilliant hues. These images open the way for a mental sensory experience of the things being compared.

Third, as we mull over the vivid images brought about by metaphors, emotional reactions arise. Concrete mental impressions of the sights and sounds of a mighty ox will create feelings of anxiety or

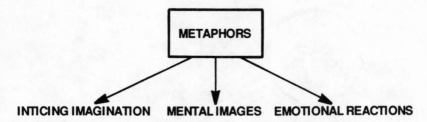

Fig. 3.3. The Functions of Metaphors

excitement. Thoughts of beautiful, rare stones create reactions of appreciation and admiration. Metaphors can move us toward a fuller response to the things being compared (see fig. 3.3).

The Psalms are rich with metaphors depicting God. The opening verses of Psalm 18 provide a powerful example. The psalmist speaks of God as "my rock," "my fortress," "my shield," "the horn of my salvation," and "my stronghold" (Ps. 18:1-2). All of these expressions are metaphorical descriptions of God. God is like a rock, like a fortress, like a shield, like a horn of salvation, and like a stronghold.

Consider the first of these comparisons. The mental picture that arises from comparing God to a rock is much more engaging than the simple statement, "God is strong and unchangeable."

One of my favorite places to visit is the rocky shore of New England. You can stand in spots where large waves crash all around but never quite reach you. How magnificent to feel so small before the sea but so secure on the solid rock. Near my desk sits a photograph in which I am perched on one of those huge rocks. That day remains vivid in my memory. I was heavily burdened by some serious problems and retreated to this place with a good friend. As we stood together before the threatening sea, my friend comforted me, saying, "God will keep you safe just as this rock keeps you safe." In the next few months, his words proved true. I still look at that photograph and find my heart comforted by the thought of God's strength against evil. God is like a rock for His people.

Scripture also pictures God metaphorically as light. His mercy and grace break into this world of sin and darkness, bringing the light of life for all who believe. Many city dwellers do not know how dark the physical world can become. Deep within a forest, when the moon and stars are hidden by the clouds, a thick darkness settles all around you—a darkness so black that you cannot even see your hand in front of your face. In such a place, a dreadful sense of being lost can easily overcome you. You frantically look about for one small glimmer of light to guide you to safety. Such an experience teaches us what it means to say that God is light. He is our salvation from the darkness of sin and death that engulfs the world.

The use of metaphors for God can create many vivid imaginative experiences that renew in us fresh fascination with God. By musing on metaphorical descriptions of God, we can enrich our awareness of Him in all of our circumstances. Metaphors for God are among the most powerful tools for deepening our contemplation of Him and discovering fascination with Him in prayer.

In this chapter we have looked into fascination with God's character. We have seen that believers need to be constantly renewed in their admiration for God. One way to fulfill this need is to contemplate God's character and to express His wonder in prayer through simple descriptions and imaginative metaphors. With just a little effort, this practice can become a vital part of every believer's communication with God.

Review Questions

1. What does it mean to be fascinated with God? In what ways can the contemplation of God's character lead to fascination with Him?

2. How can descriptions of God's character help us focus more on Him as we pray? Give a few brief descriptions that are used in biblical prayers.

3. What is a metaphor? How does it cause us to meditate on a subject? How does it create emotional responses? What are some important metaphors that may be used to describe God as we pray?

Exercises

1. Make a list of five characteristics you recognize in a person you admire. List five characteristics of God that cause you to admire Him. Describe why these qualities create admiration.

2. Choose one metaphor for God that is mentioned in this chapter. Discuss the ways this metaphor truly represents the character of God. Also discuss the emotional impact of the metaphor.

3. Write a six-to-eight-sentence prayer that focuses exclusively on the character of God (no petitions, no intercessions, etc.). As much as possible, use the following form as a guide. (See also appendices A and B.).

O Lord, You are _____
                            (Give a brief description of God.)

_____ .

You deserve all our worship and adoration. You are like _____

_____
                            (metaphor)

_____ .

We see _____
                (Describe some of the sights associated with the metaphor.)

_____

_____ ,

and we think of _____
                            (Describe a characteristic of God.)

_____ .

We hear _____
                (Describe some of the sounds associated with the metaphor.)

_____ ,

and we think of _____
                            (Describe a characteristic of God.)

_____ .

As we think on these things our hearts _____
(Describe your emotional reaction.)

_____

_____ .

We give You praise, O Lord, for You are _____

_____
(Give a brief description of God.)

_____ .

Extended Exercise

Pray at least three times this week with the exclusive purpose of describing and contemplating the character of God. Be sure to use brief descriptions and metaphors. You may find the form in exercise 3 helpful.

4

Fascination With God's Actions

In many respects our appreciation for God is also closely tied to His actions. We not only admire His character but also stand in awe of the things He does. As we have already seen, contemplating the character of God can deepen our admiration for Him. The same is true of looking at His deeds. The actions of God are so wondrous that they engender profound appreciation for Him. In this chapter, we will discuss how prayerful reflection on the acts of God leads to fascination th Him.

Contemplating the Actions of God

A keynote of biblical history is that God reveals His character through His deeds. God always acts in harmony with His nature. For this reason, when we consider the attributes of God, our minds easily move toward His actions. Psalm 36:5-9 illustrates this progression:

> Your love, O LORD, reaches to the heavens,
>   your faithfulness to the skies.

Your righteousness is like the mighty mountains,
    your justice like the great deep.
O LORD, you preserve both man and beast.
    How priceless is your unfailing love!
Both high and low among men
    find refuge in the shadow of your wings.
They feast on the abundance of your house;
    you give them drink from your river of delights.
For with you is the fountain of life;
    in your light we see light.

In the first four lines of this passage, the psalmist notes the magnificence of God's character. He compares God's lovingkindness, faithfulness, and righteousness to the mountains. He likens God's
judgments to the depths of the sea. In brief, the attributes of God are
beyond comparison. From the psalmist's perspective, the glory of
God fills the universe.

Why is he so astounded with God? What has led him to such
conclusions? We find the answer in the lines that follow. The psalmist turns from considering the character of God to reflecting on His
actions. He notes that God providentially cares for all forms of life,
protecting His people as a bird protects her young and giving
provisions of water and light to all. The psalmist does not simply
give us a still portrait of God. Rather, he describes God in action.

In the early days of cinema, no one could resist the lure of moving
pictures. Even today various kinds of motion pictures play a major
role in entertainment, education, and communication. A major
appeal of this medium is its ability to imitate the actions of life. As
wonderful as portraits and paintings may be, they cannot capture
movement which plays such an essential role in our world.

In a similar way, action is the highlight of storytelling. When we
hear someone describe episodes of a drama, we see and hear the
characters interacting with each other in their imaginative environ-
ment. This movement captures our attention and draws us into the
world of the story.

Throughout the Scriptures God is dramatically involved in the
history of the world and the lives of individuals. The Bible depicts
these activities in order to bring the glory of God into sharper focus.

A few moments of concentrating on His powerful deeds can awaken our slumbering souls. Imagining the sights and sounds of God's activity can move an indifferent, weary heart to intense astonishment with Him. For this reason, we will consider some helpful methods of focusing on the acts of God as we pray.

First, however, we must define an act of God. When believers talk about an act of God, they usually have in mind certain crucial events recorded in the Bible. We think of the creation of the world, the deliverance of Israel from Egypt, or the life, death, and resurrection of Christ. These and other dramatic events in the Bible are mighty acts of God, but God works in other ways as well. Scripture teaches that many events qualify as acts of God, not just "religious" events. All creation is God's arena. We cannot begin to name all that He does. In fact, all good things in life come from Him:

> Every good and perfect gift is from above, coming down from the Father of the heavenly lights (James 1:17a).

Even evil in the world is mysteriously restricted and used by God to accomplish His good ends:

> You intended to harm me, but God intended it for good to accomplish what is now being done, the saving of many lives (Gen. 50:20).

The eyes of faith can see God's hand everywhere. When this broad range of God's activity comes into view, the Christian must confess with the psalmist:

> Many, O LORD my God,
>   are the wonders you have done.
> The things you planned for us
>   no one can recount to you;
> were I to speak and tell of them,
>   they would be too many to declare (Ps. 40:5).

Therefore, when we turn our attention toward the actions of God, we must be ready to deal with a wide variety of events.

The story is told of a man who walked around his new neighborhood to get acquainted with the people on his block. When he came

Fig. 4.1. Two Kinds of Divine Action

to the third house on the street, he noticed a little boy, four or five years old, playing in the yard. "What's your name, son?" he asked. "My name is Billy," the boy replied. As the conversation continued the man asked, "Billy, what does your daddy do?" Billy stood up, scratched his head, and said, "My daddy shaves his face every morning!" The new neighbor could not keep from bursting out with laughter. Billy's answer was true enough, but he obviously had a limited perspective on his father's life and work.

Like Billy, Christians often view their heavenly Father from an extremely limited perspective. We narrow our appreciation for God's actions to a select few of His mighty deeds. Some believers only concentrate on the past. Others reflect only on contemporary events. Many times we think only about our own lives. Other times, we see God work only in the lives of others. To broaden our focus, we must identify the many different ways in which God acts in the world. We can do this by dividing His activities into two main categories: God's involvement in salvation history and His acts of providence (see fig. 4.1).

God's Activity in Salvation History

Throughout the Bible, we find that God intervened in the normal course of events to perform mighty acts of salvation. Though the events comprised in this salvation history are far too numerous to list here, some stand out prominently: the flood in the time of Noah, the migrations of the patriarchs, the crossing of the Red Sea, the giving of the law at Sinai, the conquest of the land, the establishment of the monarchy, the exile, the return from exile, the earthly ministry of Christ, the outpouring of the Spirit, and the return of Christ. These and many more events in the Bible accomplish salvation in a world condemned by sin to death. Obviously, these events occurred over a long period of time. God has acted, is acting, and will act with saving power in the world. For this reason, we may reflect on the past, present, and future actions of God in salvation history as we pray (see fig. 4.2).

Ancient events are the subject of many prayers in the Bible. Psalm 77:11-20 is an instructive example:

> I will remember the deeds of the LORD;
>> yes, I will remember your miracles of long ago.
> I will meditate on all your works
>> and consider all your mighty deeds.
>
> Your ways, O God, are holy.
>> What god is so great as our God?
> You are the God who performs miracles;
>> you display your power among the peoples.
> With your mighty arm you redeemed your people,
>> the descendants of Jacob and Joseph.
>
> The waters saw you, O God,
>> the waters saw you and writhed;
>> the very depths were convulsed.
> The clouds poured down water,
>> the skies resounded with thunder;
>> your arrows flashed back and forth.
> Your thunder was heard in the whirlwind,
>> your lightning lit up the world;
>> the earth trembled and quaked.
> Your path led through the sea,
>> your way through the mighty waters,
>> though your footprints were not seen.
>
> You led your people like a flock
>> by the hand of Moses and Aaron.

| PAST | PRESENT | FUTURE |

SALVATION HISTORY

Fig. 4.2. Dimensions of Salvation History

In this passage the psalmist states explicitly that he will meditate on works God performed in the past. As a result, he develops a strong sense of amazement with God. He knows that no other god can compare to the Lord. He acknowledges that God has shown great power in the redemption of Israel. Then he turns to one of the most crucial events in the entire Old Testament, the crossing of the Red Sea. With detailed imagery, the psalmist tells how God brought the people across. His description compels us to share in his excitement. The event comes alive as we read about the writhing waters, the whirlwind, the thunder, the trembling ground, and the dry path through the sea. By recounting this ancient act of God, the psalmist experienced an attitude of worship and adoration much like that of the people who actually participated in the event. Through careful contemplation, the psalmist appreciated the wonder of this act of God centuries after the event took place.

The same practice is for believers today. The Bible gives detailed accounts of many events of old. Any of these stories can become the object of deep reflection in prayer. Sadly, however, we seldom spend much time in prayer pondering these ancient acts of God.

Have you ever wondered why we do not have a book in the Bible devoted solely to Jesus' teaching? Instead, we have Gospels, which set Christ's message in the context of His many actions. The reason for this is plain. God does not want us simply to learn Christ's teaching; He also wants us to remember the details of things He did. We often miss the point. For instance, while Christians frequently mention Christ's death in prayer, they seldom take much time to reflect deeply on it. Usually, we simply thank God for sending Christ to die for our sins. A detailed remembrance of that event, however, will move our hearts to a richer appreciation for God's love manifested in the death of Christ.

Think about the cross. Scripture records Christ's humiliation and suffering in detail so that we will never forget. We see His scourged back, His thorny crown, and the blood flowing from His hands and feet. We hear the ridicule of the crowd, the pounding of the nails, the weeping of Jesus' mother, and His cries of pain. All of these events happened so that we might be redeemed from our sins. Consequently, we must take time to see, hear, and feel them in our hearts.

Praying about the death and resurrection of Christ or some other special event in His earthly ministry is one of my favorite prayer exercises. Leading groups in such prayers is always a moving experience. The sadness and horror of Christ's death pierces our hearts when we meditate on the pain of the Savior. But the joy and exhilaration of the resurrection removes life's heavy burdens from our shoulders when we think on the empty tomb.

A friend once told me that his prayer group had become dry and boring, so he decided to have the group pray in detail about Christ's death and resurrection. Afterwards he wrote to say that the exercise had transformed their prayer time into an extraordinary experience of God's blessing. Detailed prayers about these or other saving events of old can stir our hearts to worshipful appreciation and adoration for God.

The Psalms, however, do not only speak of God's saving deeds in the past. They also focus on the experience of salvation in the present. For instance, in Psalm 18:35-43 we read:

> You give me your shield of victory,
>   and your right hand sustains me;
>   you stoop down to make me great.
> You broaden the path beneath me,
>   so that my ankles do not turn.
>
> I pursued my enemies and overtook them;
>   I did not turn back till they were destroyed.
> I crushed them so that they could not rise;
>   they fell beneath my feet.
> You armed me with strength for battle;
>   you made my adversaries bow at my feet.
> You made my enemies turn their backs in flight,
>   and I destroyed my foes.

> They cried for help, but there was no one to save them—
> to the LORD, but he did not answer.
> I beat them as fine as dust borne on the wind;
> I poured them out like mud in the streets.
>
> You have delivered me from the attacks of the people;
> you have made me the head of nations;
> people I did not know are subject to me.

This passage is a prayerful reflection on God's deliverance of David from the hand of Saul. The psalmist's detail in describing the events is striking. We can see and hear the pursuit of David. We sense the frustration of Saul and his men, and we rejoice in the humiliation of David's enemies before him. As the psalmist meditates on these events, they move his heart to astonishment with God:

> The LORD lives! Praise be to my Rock!
> Exalted be God my Savior! (Ps. 18:46).

Christians today can also see the saving acts of God. All around us, we witness countless examples of God's saving His people. God is still involved in the redemption of the troubled and lost. When someone first believes or a Christian receives special help with a problem, we can be sure that God is responsible. Frequently, we may mention a word of thanks for such events, but we must move beyond this to a detailed account that can draw us into fascination with God. As the psalmist illustrates so well, careful meditation on God's contemporary saving activity can be a valuable dimension of prayer.

Finally, the prayers of the Psalms also point to the future saving acts of God. Psalm 46:8-10 gives us a beautiful picture of future events:

> Come and see the works of the LORD,
> the desolations he has brought on the earth.
> He makes wars cease to the ends of the earth;
> he breaks the bow and shatters the spear,
> he burns the shields with fire.
> "Be still, and know that I am God;
> I will be exalted among the nations,
> I will be exalted in the earth."

In these words, the psalmist anticipates the glory of the world to come. It will be a time of judgment and peace when God displays His lordship perfectly and completely. Once again, we can sense the care with which the psalmist describes these events. Reading these words, we see the broken bows and spears. The graphic description of the future creates a vivid foretaste of the event to come.

This focus on the future can be a part of our prayers today. We too wait for God to bring judgment and peace to the world. We look forward to the day when Christ will return and bring salvation in its fullness. Scripture gives us wondrous visions of that event. The appearance of Christ in the sky, the blast of the trumpet, and the resurrection of all humanity for judgment can be central to our prayers as we reflect on the future acts of God. As we take time to describe these events, our hearts will be caught up in the wonder of God.

Reflection on God's saving activity can be threefold: concern with events in the past, present, and future. As we immerse ourselves in these events, they will lead us further into an experience of fascination with God.

God's Activity in Providence

God's involvement in the world does not stop with His mighty acts of redemption. Moment by moment He providentially sustains the whole universe. Creation, sustenance, and all other good things come from His hand.

The Psalms frequently celebrate the providence of God. In Psalm 104:1, for instance, we find words of astonishment:

Praise the LORD, O my soul.

O LORD my God, you are very great;
  you are clothed with splendor and majesty.

Why is the psalmist so fascinated with God? The remainder of Psalm 104 gives us his reasons. Consider only one portion of the psalm:

He makes springs pour water into the ravines;
  it flows between the mountains.

They give water to all the beasts of the field;
  the wild donkeys quench their thirst.
The birds of the air nest by the waters;
  they sing among the branches.
He waters the mountains from his upper chambers;
  the earth is satisfied by the fruit of his work.
He makes grass grow for the cattle,
  and plants for man to cultivate—
  bringing forth food from the earth:
wine that gladdens the heart of man,
  oil to make his face shine,
  and bread that sustains his heart.
The trees of the LORD are well watered,
  the cedars of Lebanon that he planted.
There the birds make their nests;
  the stork has its home in the pine trees.
The high mountains belong to the wild goats;
  the crags are a refuge for the coneys (vv. 10-18).

In this passage, the psalmist demonstrates that his attitude toward God results from a contemplation of His acts of providence. He takes time to give a detailed account of God's providence in nature.

When I taught small children in church, I prepared the same activity every Mother's Day and Father's Day. We spent the whole session listing the things parents do for their children. At first, items came up slowly. Most children do not think much about what their parents do for them. After a few moments, however, the children began to shout ideas faster than I could write them down. It soon became apparent that mothers and fathers do many things that may not come to mind at first but constitute vital care for their children. In many ways, the same is true of God's providential care for us. On a daily basis we notice only a few of God's provisions, but when we take the time to think about them, the list grows longer and longer.

Each day we see God's providential care all around us. His blessings cannot be numbered. Sometimes they are rather spectacular—relief from a financial hardship, healing of a serious disease, protection from an accident. At other times we notice God's care in the more ordinary affairs of life—food at the supermarket, water to drink, electricity in our homes. We never have to look far to notice

Fig. 4.3. God's Extensive Providence

the kind hand of divine providence.

From the example of the Psalms, we can see the value of detailed contemplation of God's providential actions in our lives. Reflection on the providence of God in vivid and compelling detail can stir our hearts to an ever-increasing astonishment with Him. We may describe, for instance, the complexities of living organisms. Even the workings of a single cell display the splendor of God's providence. We may reflect on the delicate balance of nature and see the hand of God. We may also look at events in our personal lives. God frequently arranges our circumstances in ways that benefit us greatly. When we consider these and other expressions of God's providence, we can see anew how wondrous He is (see fig. 4.3).

In this chapter, we have looked at the importance of contemplating the actions of God in prayer. From examples of biblical prayers we have discovered the value of concrete reflection on God's acts of salvation and providence. As we put these ideas into practice, our prayers will become avenues for experiencing fascination with God.

Review Questions

1. How is God's character related to His actions? What is the value of contemplating God in "moving pictures"?

2. What are the three main dimensions of God's activity in salvation history? Give an example of a saving act of God that we tend to ignore.

3. What are some dimensions of God's activity in providence? Give an example of how we often ignore the importance of this aspect of God's action.

Exercises

1. List two great events in world history. Describe the details of each event in two or three minutes.

2. Choose one episode in the ministry of Jesus. Describe the sequence of events in detail. Tell about the sights, sounds, etc., of the episode.

3. Focusing on an event in the Bible, write a six-to-eight-sentence prayer exclusively describing God's activity (no petitions, no intercessions, etc.). As much as possible, use the form below as a guide.

O Lord of mercy and salvation, we remember Your mighty work in _____
(Name an event.)

_____

_____. We see
(Describe the sights of the event in detail.)

_____

_____

_____.

We hear _____
(Describe the sounds of the event in detail.)

_____

_____.

As we think on these things, our hearts _____

_____
(Describe your emotional reaction.)

_____.

We give You thanks, O Lord, for this Your mighty work.

Extended Exercise

Choose another episode in the Bible or a work of God in your life. At least three times this week, in prayer carefully describe examples of God's activity. Be sure to avoid petitions. You may find the form in exercise 3 helpful.

5

Seeking the Presence of God

Behold the Throne of grace!
The promise calls me near:
There Jesus shows a smiling face,
And waits to answer prayer.

John Newton
1725-1807

"Why does God seem so far away?" a man asks himself. "I used to think of Jesus as my best friend. Now I feel as if I hardly know Him." At one time or another every believer wanders through the dry desert of feeling far from God. Usually the experience lasts only a short while, but sometimes we can go for weeks, months, even years without the confidence that God is near us. In the preceding chapters, we discussed the necessity of developing a servant's attitude and a heart of fascination when coming before God in prayer. In this chapter, we will look at how prayer brings us into the presence of God.

The Nearness of God

Before examining the ways prayer can give the believer a sense of God's nearness, we must carefully define what we mean by the presence or nearness of God. The Bible speaks of God's presence in many ways, ranging from the general to the more specific. We will

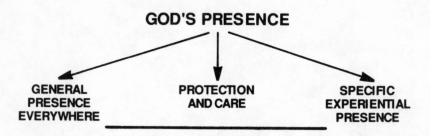

Fig. 5.1. Senses of God's Presence

look at three levels in this range of meaning: God's universal presence, His protective care, and our experiential communion with Him (see fig. 5.1).

First, we think of God as being everywhere. Little children frequently ask their parents, "Where is God?" Usually the parents respond with the simple answer, "God is everywhere." All Christians agree that God is omnipresent. He is in all places at all times. In Jeremiah we read:

> "Am I only a God nearby,"
>   declares the LORD,
>   "and not a God far away?
> Can anyone hide in secret places
>   so that I cannot see him?"
>   declares the LORD.
> "Do not I fill heaven and earth?"
>   declares the LORD (Jer. 23:23-24).

Similarly, Paul told the Athenians:

> "For in him we live and move and have our being." As some of your own poets have said, "We are his offspring" (Acts 17:28).

In one sense God cannot be limited to one place for He is everywhere.

Second, the Bible also speaks of God's presence in terms of His protection and care for believers. For instance, Jacob prayed that God would be with him as he ran from his brother Esau (Gen. 28:20-21). Joseph's success in Egypt was attributed to the fact that

God was with him (Gen. 39:2). Similarly, Jesus Himself promised that He would be with the apostles as they carried out His Great Commission (Matt. 28:20). As Psalm 46:1-2 puts it:

> God is our refuge and strength,
>   an ever present help in trouble.
> Therefore we will not fear, though the earth give way
>   and the mountains fall into the heart of the sea.

According to the psalmist, God is present with us even in trouble. He is there to help. So it is that the presence of God also is the protective care He gives His servants.

Third, in many portions of the Bible, Scripture speaks of God's presence in the sense of experiential communion with Him. We read, for instance, of God walking in the Garden of Eden in the cool of the day (Gen. 3:8). On the day of Pentecost the Holy Spirit came upon the apostles in an immediate and personal way (Acts 2:1-4). When Solomon completed the temple in Jerusalem, he recognized that, although God could not be contained within its walls, the worshipers could experience a special nearness to God in the temple:

> May your eyes be open toward this temple night and day, this place of which you said, "My Name shall be there," so that you will hear the prayer your servant prays toward this place (1 Kings 8:29).

In the days of the Old Testament, the temple was the place in which God chose to dwell in a special way. It was the site where believers could encounter God intimately through the varied experiences of worship.

Several distinctive features of experiential communion with God become apparent when we contrast it with God's omnipresence. Unlike God's general presence everywhere, the *experience* of God's nearness comes and goes. Moreover, on the occasions when Christians experience this special presence, He comes near in ways that cannot be ignored. In this special sense God's presence is a divine-human encounter that deeply affects believers.

Today, prayer is one of the most valuable avenues to sensing the experiential dimension of God's nearness. While we no longer walk with God in the Garden of Eden or see the tongues of fire at Pentecost, we are able to encounter God through prayer. By talking with Him, we are given the opportunity to experience His special presence. Such communion with God has a powerful result. When we come close to God, He touches us at the deepest levels of our being.

This dimension of God's nearness is not entirely foreign to ordinary human experience. We have similar times with special people we encounter. I remember the first time I met one of my Old Testament professors in graduate school. This professor was recognized worldwide as one of the best in his field. As a young seminary graduate meeting him for the first time, I was very nervous, to say the least. During the few moments we had together that day, I could hardly speak a complete sentence because I knew that I was with someone who was by far my superior. It was no ordinary experience. Similarly, few of us would remain calm if we were invited to have dinner with the president of the United States. We would find it difficult to eat and carry on a calm conversation while sitting with the leader of our nation. If meeting with mere humans can affect us so, how much greater the effect when meeting with Divinity! Communion with God cannot be brushed aside and forgotten as if it were an ordinary experience. It sparks a fire at the core of our being that consumes us.

People react differently to the presence of God, but two attitudes consistently occur in the hearts of those who enter into His special presence. On the one hand, a person may be struck with an overwhelming sense of humility. In the presence of God, we realize our inadequacy as creatures and sinners. Adam and Eve hid from God as He approached. The Israelites bowed low before Him in His temple. As Isaiah met with God in the temple, his first words were:

> "Woe to me!" I cried. "I am ruined! For I am a man of unclean lips, and I live among a people of unclean lips, and my eyes have seen the King, the LORD Almighty" (Isa. 6:5).

As we draw near to God, we encounter God's surpassing glory, and we are humbled.

On the other hand, in the special presence of God, we may

discover the satisfaction and joy of being accepted by Him. God's receptivity calms troubled hearts and fills them with excitement and joy. Temple worshipers were encouraged to sing praises and to dance in the wonder of God's special presence. People accused the apostles of drunkenness because of their joy before the Lord at Pentecost. Even Isaiah discovered a new confidence before God:

> Then I heard the voice of the Lord saying, "Whom shall I send? And who will go for us?" And I said, "Here am I. Send me!" (Isa. 6:8).

Experiencing the intimate presence of God can humble, assure, comfort, and uplift us. Whatever our reaction may be at a particular moment, the nearness of God cannot be ignored. We are profoundly grasped by the power of God and quickened into a fuller awareness of Him and our relationship to Him.

A Desire for God's Presence

All Christians want to know God in a close, personal way, but often this desire is not fulfilled. We frequently hear believers say, "God never seems close to me. Is He really listening to my prayers?" We lack assurance that God is intimately concerned with us. Yet, followers of Christ are never satisfied to stay in this condition for long. A husband and wife who are in a happy marriage can be separated for a time, but soon they will begin to miss each other. The same is true of believers and their God. From time to time we manage without a sense of God's nearness, but a continuation of that state is unsatisfying. True believers yearn to be close to God and to feel the assurance of His personal attention.

Psalm 73:25-28a illustrates how intense a longing for God's presence can become:

> Whom have I in heaven but you?
>> And being with you, I desire nothing on earth.
> My flesh and my heart may fail,
>> but God is the strength of my heart
>> and my portion forever.

Those who are far from you will perish;
    you destroy all who are unfaithful to you.
But as for me, it is good to be near God.

In this passage the psalmist reflects on his great need for God. As long as he can be near God, he needs nothing else. Even if his body should fail him, the psalmist affirms that he finds his strength in God. Unbelievers are far from God, and their end will surely be destruction. The psalmist, however, looks to God as a refuge from the turmoil and dangers of life. In fact, His highest goal is to have an awareness of God's nearness. This same goal is shared by all believers.

Why then do we often end up feeling distant from God? What causes this experience of separation from Him? Often, we must simply acknowledge that we do not know why God seems distant. At times, His ways remain inscrutable. Nevertheless, the two greatest obstacles to intimacy with God are sin and a neglect of God.

Willful, continual sin erects a barrier between humans and God. Even as believers, we suffer a sense of separation because of sin. This is why we confess our transgressions. Confession opens com--munion between God and His people. From time to time we must all seek restoration with God. As David prayed after his adultery,

Restore to me the joy of your salvation (Ps. 51:12a).

It is not unusual for pastors to face this problem among their church members. I remember several occasions when I have heard believers ask, "Why do I feel that God is so far away?" As troubling as it may be, our response to this question must raise the matter of sin. "Is there some serious sin that keeps you from God?" I would ask. So it is for all of us. When we desire to be near to God, we must confess our sins and turn away from practices that block our relationship with Him.

And yet, conscious sin is not always the problem. We do not have to be in deep sin to feel distant from God. Sometimes we may confess our sins, try to live holy lives, and still not sense His nearness. Why is this so? Many different problems may lie behind this experience, but one reason is our frequent neglect of God in prayer.

We have a similar kind of experience with other human beings.

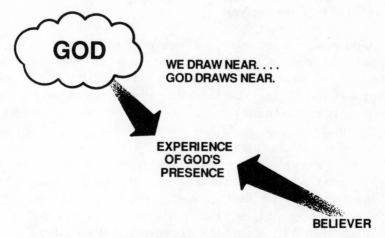

Fig. 5.2. Drawing Near to God

Most teen-agers have suffered the agony of having a date with someone they did not like very much. Even adults occasionally have to spend time with someone they would rather avoid. Generally we respond to these situations by putting a psychological distance between ourselves and the other person. We remain uninterested in what he or she says and keep our conversation on the most super-ficial level. But when we are with someone we like very much, we put our hearts into the conversation and pay close attention to that person. We not only share the same space; we also share ourselves with each other.

In many respects the same principles apply to our conversations with God. If we ignore God in our prayers, we cannot expect Him to bless us with an awareness of His special presence. James puts the matter succinctly:

Come near to God and he will come near to you (James 4:8a).

Notice the order of events. If we want to experience the presence of God, we must draw near to Him. In other words, we must seek after God as we pray. We must devote our hearts to communing with Him in a vibrant and personal way. If we do this, we can expect God to respond by drawing near to us. He will reciprocate with intimate attention and blessing (see fig. 5.2).

Avenues for Drawing Near

God has ordained many avenues for drawing near to Him in prayer. In previous chapters, we have looked in some detail at the two vital elements of contemplating God's character and actions. These kinds of focus on God are vital paths for drawing near. As we put our hearts and minds on God, we come ever closer to Him in the communion of prayer. At this point, however, we will explore another way of drawing near.

One of the greatest privileges believers have is the freedom to approach God in His heavenly dwelling place through prayer. Christians often complain that their prayers never seem to go beyond the ceiling. It is as if our words stay tied to earth and never reach heaven. Yet, we should not be surprised at this. After all, how often do we even concern ourselves with the heights of heaven when we pray? How frequently do we contemplate the dwelling place of God? As long as our minds are focused exclusively on the things of this realm, we should not be surprised when we lack confidence that our prayers reach heaven. Yet, when we lift our hearts to heaven, we can discover an ever-increasing assurance that our prayers are reaching God and that He is giving us His personal attention.

We find a focus on God's heavenly dwelling throughout the Bible. In fact, descriptions of God's activities in heaven are quite detailed at times. The opening chapter of Job depicts God sitting in His throne room with angelic beings coming and going before Him (Job 1:6-12). Dialogue ensues between the divine King and His audience; decrees are issued and obeyed. Many Old Testament prophets experienced visions of heaven and related what they saw in prophetic messages (Isa. 6:1-13; 1 Kings 22:19; Dan. 7:9-11). These and many other passages portray heaven as a royal palace with God as the enthroned King. He is surrounded by an attentive audience of heavenly beings who respond to His bidding. The words of Daniel are particularly striking:

As I looked,

thrones were set in place,
and the Ancient of Days took his seat.

His clothing was as white as snow;
   the hair of his head was white like wool.
His throne was flaming with fire,
   and its wheels were all ablaze.
A river of fire was flowing,
   coming out from before him.
Thousands upon thousands attended him;
   ten thousand times ten thousand stood before him.
The court was seated,
   and the books were opened (Dan. 7:9-10).

In the New Testament, we read about Stephen's glimpse of heaven (Acts 7:55-56). The book of Revelation also offers a glorious portrait of the heavenly realms:

At once I was in the Spirit, and there before me was a throne in heaven with someone sitting on it. And the one who sat there had the appearance of jasper and carnelian. A rainbow, resembling an emerald, encircled the throne. Surrounding the throne were twenty-four other thrones, and seated on them were twenty-four elders. They were dressed in white and had crowns of gold on their heads. From the throne came flashes of lightning, rumblings and peals of thunder. Before the throne, seven lamps were blazing. These are the seven spirits of God. Also before the throne there was what looked like a sea of glass, clear as crystal.

In the center, around the throne, were four living creatures, and they were covered with eyes, in front and in back. The first living creature was like a lion, the second was like an ox, the third had a face like a man, the fourth was like a flying eagle. Each of the four living creatures had six wings and was covered with eyes all around, even under his wings (Rev. 4:2-8a).

In all of these passages, the picture of heaven is similar—a magnificent royal court filled with unimaginable splendor and glory. Unlike most Christians today, believers living during the days of the Bible used many rich images of heaven. Of course, these images were but glimpses into realms far beyond human comprehension. Yet, when the biblical writers thought about heaven, they did not—as we often do—stare blankly into empty space. They had a firm conception of heaven. It was the splendid palace of the divine King of Israel, God Himself.

A focus on God in heaven is an important facet of many biblical prayers. In Psalm 102:19 we read,

> The LORD looked down from his sanctuary on high,
> from heaven he viewed the earth.

This psalm pictures God in His heavenly dwelling, high above all creation, looking down upon His subjects on earth. We find similar portraits in other psalms (Pss. 53:2; 33:13). Modern readers frequently skim over these words; their lack of concern with heaven keeps them from seeing what the words portray. But if we attend to the rich images of heaven that lie behind the words, we begin to realize that these vignettes represent a vast complex of ideas regarding heaven and God's activity there.

One excellent example of reflection on heaven can be found in Psalm 104:1-4:

> Praise the LORD, O my soul.
>
> O LORD my God, you are very great;
> you are clothed with splendor and majesty.
> He wraps himself in light as with a garment;
> he stretches out the heavens like a tent
> and lays the beams of his upper chambers on their waters.
> He makes the clouds his chariot
> and rides on the wings of the wind.
> He makes winds his messengers,
> flames of fire his servants.

Notice the detail of the psalmist's description. He speaks of God's clothing. He reflects on the construction of God's dwelling place. He describes His cloud chariot and His messengers, wind and fire. With only a cursory look at this passage, we can see that the psalmist is intensely concerned with the details of heaven. The sights and sounds of heaven captivate his heart. His mind stretches for words to express his amazement at the divine dwelling. Although the psalmist describes heaven in the human terms of clothing, chambers, chariots, and messengers, he knows that nothing in this world

can begin to match this scene. Such reflection has lifted the psalmist's imagination out of the world and set it in the dwelling place of
God.

Can our prayers today have the same focus? Can we also look into
heaven and see God's activity there? In two ways the answer to this
question must be no. First, with the completion of the canon of
Scripture, we should no longer expect to receive revelations from
God as the prophets of old. Our knowledge of God and His will
must be guided by Scripture. In this sense, we should not even seek
to be privy to the heavenly realms. What we need to know about
God and His will has been revealed in sacred Scripture. Second, we
must not identify our imaginative reflections on heaven too closely
with reality. God has commanded that we make no graven images
of Him (Exod. 20:4). This command also includes thinking that our
mental concepts fully capture God. We must always remember that
we still "see but a poor reflection" (1 Cor. 13:12).

Even so, these qualifications do not imply that Christians should
avoid all reflection on heaven. On the contrary, we are commanded
by Scripture to set our minds there:

> Since, then, you have been raised with Christ, set your hearts
> on things above, where Christ is seated at the right hand of
> God (Col. 3:1).

Paul's exhortation is clear. We should contemplate those things
above, not those things below. The Lord's Prayer also instructs us to
focus on heaven:

> Our Father *in heaven* . . .
> your will be done
>   on earth as it is *in heaven* (Matt. 6:9, 10).

Often believers forget that this world is only temporary. With heavy
chains we bind our hearts to the things of this life, even in our
prayers. We only pray about what is happening here and forget to
turn our mind's eye toward heaven.

Contemplation of heaven can be a fruitful prayer experience.
Imagine the throne room of God: the splendid sights and sounds of
the host surrounding the throne, the brilliant light radiating from

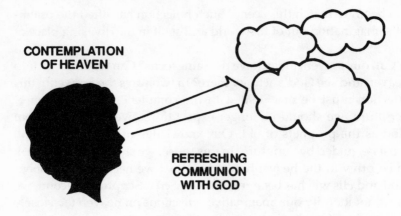

Fig. 5.3. Contemplating Heaven

the throne itself. We see Christ, who is seated next to the Father, rise to make intercession. In our hearts we are there. We hear the praises of angelic creatures crying, "Holy, Holy, Holy." What can we do but fall to the ground? We are overcome by the majesty of it all, overwhelmed with inexpressible reverence. What can we do but rejoice? We are caught up in rapturous exhilaration, kneeling in the very presence of God. So long as we are guided by the teaching of Scripture, prayerful reflection on heavenly scenes can lead us into a wondrous experience of God's nearness. Filling our prayers with detailed reflection on God in heaven can take our hearts away from this world of death and bathe them in refreshing communion with God (see fig. 5.3).

In this chapter we have looked at the benefits of focusing on God's dwelling place. Reflection on His character, His actions, and His dwelling place in our prayers can bless us with a sense that we are close to God and that He is close to us.

Review Questions

1. In what senses does the Bible speak of the presence of God? How are these senses different? How are they similar?

2. Why should Christians desire to experience special intimacy with God? What benefits can we find in the experience?

3. How can Christians draw near to God in prayer? How can the contemplation of heaven be a way of drawing close to God?

Exercises

1. Look at Daniel 7:9-10 and Revelation 4:2-8. Make a list of at least five heavenly realities you see and hear. Describe how wondrous these things are in heaven.

2. Write a six-to-eight-sentence prayer that focuses exclusively on the wonder of God in heaven (no petitions, no intercessions, etc.). As much as possible, use the form below as a guide.

O _____ , heaven
                            (divine name or title)

is full of Your glory, glory beyond imagination. We see _____

_____
                    (Describe some sights of heaven.)

_____ ,

and we feel _____
                            (Describe your emotional reaction.)

_____ .

As we think of Your heavenly dwelling, we hear _____

_____
                    (Describe some sounds of heaven.)

_____ ,

and we feel _____
                            (Describe your emotional reaction.)

_____ .

Glory be to the Lord our God who calls us to come into His presence.
His mercy is everlasting. Amen.

Extended Exercise

During the next week spend two or three times in prayer focusing on God in His heavenly dwelling without asking for anything. Also try to incorporate descriptions of His character and His actions. You may find it helpful to use the form suggested above in exercise 2.

Part Two

LOOKING AT
OURSELVES

6

Praying Between the Times

I'm but a stranger here,
Heaven is my home;
Earth is a desert drear,
Heaven is my home:
Danger and sorrow stand
Round me on every hand;
Heaven is my fatherland,
Heaven is my home.
                    Thomas R. Taylor
                    1807-35

Do you sometimes feel that prayer has nothing to do with real life? After all, we live in a modern world that has little patience with people who pray. At times the world's cynicism leads us to doubt that communication with God has any bearing on our lives. Without realizing it, such doubts tempt us to abandon prayer in favor of activities that seem more productive, like studying the Bible, evangelizing, or ministering to the poor. So why waste time in prayer?

The Bible teaches that prayer is immensely relevant. It is not time wasted but a crucial ingredient in our walk with Christ.

In this chapter, we will begin to explore how the Bible presents the relevance of prayer for the modern world. In many ways, the key to this issue is to discover how prayer relates to different aspects of our lives and how it fits in moments of happiness, joy, sadness, grief, and pain. For this reason, we will turn our attention toward the second element in our definition—the believer as the source of prayer.

The Christian Experience

An awareness of the different dimensions of Christian experience is essential for understanding the relevance of prayer. God has ordained prayer as a way to communicate with Him in every circumstance. So we must take a close look at the many facets of our experience. Learning about prayer in all these conditions will reveal its great relevance for each of us.

God's master plan for the history of the world has produced a great diversity within humanity. People in the Far East, in Scandinavia, and in Africa differ greatly from each other. The climates, social customs, and economic systems of these places play major roles in creating this variety. Even within the same culture, people have different personal backgrounds. A unique set of experiences has made each of us different from those around us. Nevertheless, some features of life are common to all people. If nothing else, we all live, eat food, drink water, breathe the air, sleep, and eventually die. These and other common experiences form a backdrop against which we may appreciate the diversity of the human race.

The Christian life also exhibits unity and diversity. All believers have unique experiences, which contribute significantly to who they are. Some belong to one denomination, and others to another. Some go through life in poverty, and others in wealth. Some are free from psychological problems, and others are plagued with lifelong emotional difficulties. Our diverse backgrounds set the stage for many differences among us.

Nevertheless, certain experiences are common to all believers. In the New Testament we learn that the Christian life is largely molded by the character of the times in which we live. Because we serve God in the period between the first and second comings of Christ, we all have vital connections with both the past and the future. The cross is the basis for our hope in the promises of God, but not until the return of Christ will all these promises be fully realized. For this reason, every Christian's life is both a time of great *blessing* and a time of much *waiting*.

When my wife and I first learned that we were expecting a child, we were filled with delight. The thought of new life growing inside her drew us closer than we had ever been before. I remember clearly

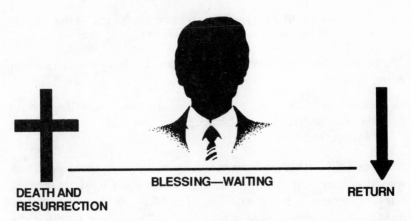

DEATH AND   **BLESSING—WAITING**   **RETURN**
RESURRECTION

Fig. 6.1. Two Sides of the Christian Life

the morning when the doctor permitted me to hear my daughter's heartbeat for the first time. What a thrill! Although the nine months were filled with happiness, they were also full of difficulties. By the seventh and eighth months, we were eager for our child to be born. The days and nights dragged on and on, and our hearts turned with great longing toward the delivery day. Knowing a child will be born can be a great blessing, but it can also be a long period of waiting.

The entire Christian life is like expecting a child. Many joys are ours in this life now, but we look forward to a better day to come. This tension between blessing and waiting is common to all Christians (see fig. 6.1).

To live after the resurrection of Christ is to share in many blessings from God. When Christ's work was accomplished, great gifts were bestowed. The Old Testament looked forward to the day of Christ as a time of mercy and salvation for the world. In His earthly work, Jesus began to fulfill those Old Testament hopes and span the gulf that once separated us from God:

> Consequently, you are no longer foreigners and aliens, but fellow citizens with God's people and members of God's household (Eph. 2:19).

Our guilt has been laid upon Christ, and His righteousness has become ours:

> God made him who had no sin to be sin for us, so that in him
> we might become the righteousness of God (2 Cor. 5:21).

The results of Christ's work are wondrous. We have been blessed in
many ways:

> Praise be to the God and Father of our Lord Jesus Christ, who
> has blessed us in the heavenly realms with every spiritual
> blessing in Christ (Eph. 1:3).

At certain times these blessings are especially precious to us. When
we suffer from guilt, we are relieved to know that Christ has secured
our forgiveness. When we undergo hardship, we are comforted by
the Spirit. When we have physical needs, we praise God for His
provisions. When we feel powerless in this world, we are strengthened to know that God has already seated us with Christ. In one
way or another, every believer knows some dimension of blessing in
this age. The blessings of living after the first coming of Christ
extend to us all.

Nevertheless, life in our age is also a time of waiting. While
Christ accomplished much for us in His first coming, we still live
before the completion of His saving work. We yearn for the return of
Christ because sin still troubles us. At times sinful tendencies create
immeasurable inner conflict:

> So I say, live by the Spirit, and you will not gratify the desires of
> the sinful nature. For the sinful nature desires what is contrary
> to the Spirit, and the Spirit what is contrary to the sinful nature.
> They are in conflict with each other, so that you do not do what
> you want (Gal. 5:16-17).

We also wait to see the judgment of God against wickedness and the
reward for righteousness:

> God is just: He will pay back trouble to those who trouble you
> and give relief to you who are troubled, and to us as well. This
> will happen when the Lord Jesus is revealed from heaven in
> blazing fire with his powerful angels. He will punish those who
> do not know God and do not obey the gospel of our Lord Jesus.
> They will be punished with everlasting destruction and shut
> out from the presence of the Lord and from the majesty of his

power on the day he comes to be glorified in his holy people and to be marveled at among all those who have believed. This includes you, because you believed our testimony to you (2 Thess. 1:6-10).

We wait for the second coming of Christ to end all the suffering, pain, and death that now characterize our existence:

Then I saw a new heaven and a new earth, for the first heaven and the first earth had passed away, and there was no longer any sea. I saw the Holy City, the new Jerusalem, coming down out of heaven from God, prepared as a bride beautifully dressed for her husband. . . . He will wipe every tear from their eyes. There will be no more death or mourning or crying or pain, for the old order of things has passed away (Rev. 21:1-2, 4).

We look for the day when the foretaste of heaven that we now have will be exchanged for our full reward in Christ.

Life is different for each of us. Yet, we know that one great tension characterizes all of our experiences. We have good and bad, relief and hardship, blessing and waiting.

Responding in Faith

How should we respond to this mixed experience? What should our attitude be as we react to the good and bad of life? Unfortunately, Christians tend to go to one extreme or the other in this matter. On the one hand, many believers are keenly aware of the waiting that characterizes their lives, placing a great deal of emphasis on the sins and troubles that continue to bother them. As a result, they become sullen, remorseful, and negative about life. Joy and excitement seldom find a path to their hearts. Even when things are going well, they fear becoming too happy because another disappointment is just around the corner.

We have to realize that becoming a Christian does not protect a person from suffering. Sometimes believers dedicate their time and money to a good cause only to see it crumble. Many Christian families go through serious problems. We are still affected by illness and death. Sadness is part of our lives. Nevertheless, sadness, depression, and other negative emotions need not be our only responses to life. Again and again, Christians suffer tremendous hardships—accidents, sickness, persecution—but testify to the comfort of God's love while going through these experiences. Events in our lives often warrant negative reactions. Yet, when we always respond to life with negative attitudes, we must ask ourselves if we have overlooked the wonder of what God has already done for us in the first coming of Christ. This is why the Scriptures tell us,

> Give thanks in all circumstances, for this is God's will for you in Christ Jesus (1 Thess. 5:18).

The grace of God is able to help us sustain many positive attitudes even in the midst of suffering.

On the other hand, many Christians mistakenly think that they should react only positively to life. These believers hold that God has already given us so much that any hardship we face is trivial. From this point of view, we should face trouble simply by saying, "Praise the Lord, anyway." Optimism is the only acceptable response to life. Becoming frustrated or sad is only for weak and worldly Christians.

This viewpoint overlooks the fact that we are still waiting for Christ to return in glory. Jesus Himself occasionally reacted negatively toward life. He responded to events with sadness (John 11: 33, 35, 38) and even anger (Mark 3:5). Such emotions are not always sinful. We are even commanded in one passage to be angry, though without sin (Eph. 4:26). Many situations deserve negative reactions.

Some people have a greater ability than others to see the bright side of things. We rightly admire those who can keep a positive outlook on life, even in the midst of personal suffering. Yet, we must be cautious. Often these same people treat the sorrows and pains of others with a carefree shrug of the shoulders. When this occurs, they are no longer simply positive about life. They are callous toward the pain of others. The mark of spiritual maturity is not constant happiness but knowing how to

> rejoice with those who rejoice; mourn with those who mourn (Rom. 12:15).

Fig. 6.2. Christian Response to Life

Following the example of Christ, we should recognize that negative attitudes are appropriate at times. Responding to life with positive attitudes alone demonstrates a blindness to the evil still rampant in our world.

In other words, our mixed experiences should bring mixed responses. The great blessings that are ours in Christ should cause us to rejoice and be glad. His kindness can even bring joy to our hearts in the midst of struggling and suffering. Nevertheless, a Christian response to life is to be an honest response. As life itself is negative and positive, the Christian response should be negative and positive. The well-known words from Ecclesiastes sum up the matter nicely. In God's order for life there is

> a time to weep and a time to laugh,
> a time to mourn and a time to dance (Eccl. 3:4).

(See fig. 6.2.)

Opening Up in Prayer

The two sides of Christian experience raise an important question. How are we to deal with the positive and negative dimensions of life when we pray? Is it acceptable for us to talk with God about our attitudes in all these conditions? The Bible indicates in many places that Christians must be ready to open their hearts fully before God in whatever condition they find themselves. From the Psalms, we see that openness is vital to communication with God. In fact, the relevance of prayer for everyday life becomes crystal clear when we seek to be honest with God about both our negative and our positive attitudes. We will be looking into specific dimensions of honesty in prayer in the chapters that follow, but first we must look at some preliminary considerations.

Throughout the Psalms we find that positive attitudes toward life are expressed to God through thanksgiving and praise. When good occurs, believers respond with praise. Notice the enthusiasm with which the psalmist praises God:

> I will exalt you, my God the King;
>   I will praise your name for ever and ever.
> Every day I will praise you
>   and extol your name for ever and ever.
>
> Great is the LORD and most worthy of praise;
>   his greatness no one can fathom.
> One generation will commend your works to another;
>   they will tell of your mighty acts.
> They will speak of the glorious splendor of your majesty,
>   and I will meditate on your wonderful works.
> They will tell of the power of your awesome works,
>   and I will proclaim your great deeds.
> They will celebrate your abundant goodness
>   and joyfully sing of your righteousness (Ps. 145:1-7).

The psalmist exudes joy. He exclaims that he will praise God for all time. He vows to exalt God every day. He tells us that he is excited because he has experienced the wonderful blessings of God's deeds. Finally, he pledges to meditate on the wondrous works of God, to proclaim them, and to celebrate the abundant goodness of God. Clearly, prayer can be a means through which believers express to God their positive attitudes toward life.

At the same time, however, we also find examples of negative feelings in the Psalms. When times of trouble assail the psalmists, they express their honest reactions to their situations. In Psalm 69:29 the psalmist writes,

I am in pain and distress;
  may your salvation, O God, protect me.

Why is he in such agony? From the earlier verses of the psalm we know that his pain and distress are the result of miserable experiences. He cries:

Save me, O God,
  for the waters have come up to my neck.
I sink in the miry depths,
  where there is no foothold.
I have come into the deep waters;
  the floods engulf me (vv. 1, 2).

Moreover he adds,

You know how I am scorned, disgraced and shamed;
  all my enemies are before you (v. 19).

To be sure, toward the end of the psalm the psalmist praises God (vv. 30-36). Yet, the majority of this inspired prayer expresses negative feelings. The psalmist sees himself sinking in the mire of false accusations, mockery, and shame. He must grit his teeth and wait for justice to prevail. Yet, because he knows the relevance of prayer, the psalmist spends much time pouring out his negative feelings to God. He opens himself before God and shares his complaints as well as his praises.

On one occasion I visited a church member whose family was going through some serious difficulties. The man had lost his job; finances were in shambles; it even seemed that his wife might leave him. While he and I talked, his agony and pain were apparent. With a remorseful heart, he told me how he had done his best but found that circumstances were simply too great for him to overcome. Afterwards, I asked him to join me in prayer. As he began to speak to God, his tone of voice changed completely. He put on a happy face and began to thank God for His blessings and care. His whole demeanor remained upbeat through the prayer. Then, immediately after the prayer, he fell back into his previous mood. Words of sadness and frustration poured from his lips. Then I realized that when this man began to pray, he had shifted into automatic pilot.

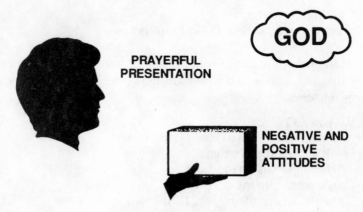

Fig. 6.3. Attitudes in Prayer

His prayer had little to do with what was in his heart. It merely followed his preconception of a "good prayer." Sadly, many of us pray the same way because we think that only positive attitudes of joy, peace, and thanksgiving are acceptable in prayer. No wonder prayer seems so irrelevant.

God does not expect us to withhold our honest responses to life. As the psalmists expressed positive and negative attitudes in their prayers, we may do the same. Before we approach God in prayer, we should examine our attitudes. How do we feel about God, the world around us, and ourselves? From time to time, we will find that we have positive and negative reactions to all these dimensions of life. Whatever the case, these attitudes toward life should then be laid before God in prayer (see fig. 6.3).

Christians live between the first and second comings of Christ. As a result, our lives are characterized by blessing and waiting. Prayer should reflect both sides of this condition. Indeed, when we openly express ourselves to God, we throw wide the door to fruitful and relevant communication with Him.

Review Questions

1. Why is the Christian experience a time of blessing? Why is it a

time of waiting? How does this tension relate to the first and second comings of Christ?

2. How should we respond to our mixed experiences as faithful followers of Christ? Are there examples of negative and positive attitudes in the life of Christ?

3. How can prayer be a time when we open up before God? What biblical support is there for expressing positive and negative attitudes in prayer?

Exercises

1. List five blessings you have received as the result of the death and resurrection of Christ. Also list five things you are waiting to receive from Christ.

2. Take the lists of exercise 1 and choose the most positive and the most negative examples. Write a sentence expressing your attitudes toward these dimensions of your life.

3. Using the form suggested here, choose one blessing that most Christians experience and one negative dimension of life and express your attitude about them in prayer.

Lord of wondrous grace, we look to You with amazement because

_____
(Name a blessing from God.)

_____ .

When we think of this blessing, we feel _____
(Name an emotional reaction.)

_____

_____ .

How good You are to us!

Lord of compassionate love, we look to You for understanding
because _____
(Describe a negative experience.)

_____.

When we think of this experience we feel _____
(Describe a reaction.)

_____

_____.

How we need Your mercy every day. Amen.

Extended Exercise

At least three times this week, pray expressing your attitudes toward both the positive and the negative dimensions of your life. You
may find the form in exercise 3 helpful.

7

In Times of Trouble

Ah, whither could we flee for aid,
When tempted, desolate, dismayed,
Or how the hosts of hell defeat,
Had suffering saints no mercy-seat?
                    Hugh Stowell
                    1799-1865

The scene is tragic—a young African girl sits in the scorching sun, too weak to stand. Flies light unmolested on her face. Her bloated belly and sunken eyes tell the story—she is starving. It has been two days since the last smattering of pasty oatmeal, a feast under these conditions.

At last, she edges toward the makeshift clinic. A young man reaches for her hand and takes her into the tent. "I'm next for food," she thinks. "But why are they measuring me? Why are they weighing me? Just give me food!"

At the other end of the tent are two exits. Some children are sent to the left, but most are carried to the right. The little girl goes right with most of the others; she is put on a truck and driven away. No food for her or the hundreds who pass her way. When there is not enough food for everyone, the weakest are carried off and left to die. A nightmare? Yes, but for some in the world, this scene is a horrible reality.

Situations like this are hard to ignore. Even the most upbeat, happy-go-lucky person is shaken by thoughts of starving children. An assortment of feelings swells within us. We mourn over the suffering and loss of life. We are frustrated by our inability to remedy the situation. We may even wonder why God allows such cruelty.

What is the best way to handle these feelings? Is there any legitimate outlet for the troubles that plague our hearts? Along with working for solutions to problems like these, we should also turn to God in prayer. In the previous chapter, we saw that our negative emotions are a legitimate part of prayer. Now, we will establish guidelines for effectively talking with God about our troubles.

Coming as We Are

Many believers insist that Christians should be completely satisfied with their situations in life. "Make sure your attitudes are straight before you come to God," we are told. While this principle sounds good, it may actually hurt more than it helps. Time and again, examples of prayer in the Bible make it apparent that when we are troubled, God wants us to come to Him just as we are. Even when our hearts are deeply disturbed, God wants us to draw near.

Many psalms illustrate God's desire to hear us when we are burdened with life's problems. Psalm 22 indicates with striking clarity that God wants us to come before Him with our troubled hearts. The opening of this psalm is familiar to us all:

My God, my God, why have you forsaken me? (22:1a).

Countless Old Testament believers uttered these words as they suffered hardship and sensed separation from God. Today we know them well because Jesus quoted this prayer as he underwent the agony of the cross (Matt. 27:46). To be sure, Christ's suffering far exceeded the difficulties we face. On the cross, Jesus bore God's judgment for our sins—a judgment we will never have to bear because of His sacrifice. Nevertheless, Christ's sinless example shows us that prayers like Psalm 22 are valid patterns for us to follow.

In Psalm 22, the writer openly expresses many negative attitudes before God. *First*, the psalmist feels badly about himself. He looks at himself and is displeased with what he sees. Having lost all sense of personal dignity, he exclaims,

> But I am a worm and not a man (v. 6a).

He also describes his poor physical condition:

> I am poured out like water,
>   and all my bones are out of joint.
> My heart has turned to wax;
>   it has melted away within me.
> My strength is dried up like a potsherd,
>   and my tongue sticks to the roof of my mouth;
>   you lay me in the dust of death (vv. 14, 15).

We can find similar expressions in many psalms. For instance, in Psalm 55:2 we read,

> My thoughts trouble me and I am distraught.

From these examples (see also Pss. 69:2; 90:10), we can pinpoint one source of our troubles in life. We mourn over our own condition. We grieve over our disappointment and discouragement. We are frustrated and perplexed. We do not sense the dignity that is ours as creatures made in the image of God.

Second, the psalmist expresses displeasure for his outward circumstances. He tells God about the scorn he receives from other people:

> . . . scorned by men and despised by the people.
> All who see me mock me;
>   they hurl insults, shaking their heads (22:6b-7).

He describes his opponents as powerful, vicious animals:

> Many bulls surround me;
>   strong bulls of Bashan encircle me.
>
> Dogs have surrounded me;
>   a band of evil men has encircled me (22:12, 16).

We can find similar depictions of outward circumstances in other psalms as well. In Psalm 55, the psalmist claims that his troubled attitude results from the actions of those around him:

> My thoughts trouble me and I am distraught
>> at the voice of the enemy,
>> at the stares of the wicked;
> for they bring down suffering upon me
>> and revile me in their anger (vv. 2b, 3).

In our day we, too, are falsely accused; jobs are taken from us; friends betray us; accidents occur; loved ones suffer and die. All of these situations can deeply discourage us. We become sorrowful and frustrated. The Psalms teach that we should bring our frustrations with the world around us to God in prayer. He is not interested merely in what we think about ourselves. He also wants us to tell Him about our attitudes toward the bad circumstances we face.

Third, the psalmist also expresses his troubled feelings about God. Psalm 22 begins with the question, Why?

> My God, my God, *why* have you forsaken me?
>> *Why* are you so far from saving me,
>> so far from the words of my groaning?
> O my God, I cry out by day, but you do not answer,
>> by night, and am not silent (vv. 1, 2).

The main concern of these verses is God's apparent unwillingness to answer the psalmist's prayer. Although God's holiness is not doubted, from the psalmist's limited point of view, present realities stand in sharp contrast to the way God acted in the past. In the past, when Israel cried out in trouble, God answered:

> In you our fathers put their trust;
>> they trusted and you delivered them.
> They cried to you and were saved;
>> in you they trusted and were not disappointed (vv. 4-5).

In the psalmist's life, however, God seems silent and inactive. The psalmist's dismay is amplified by his long relationship with God:

> From birth I was cast upon you;
>> from my mother's womb you have been my God (v. 10).

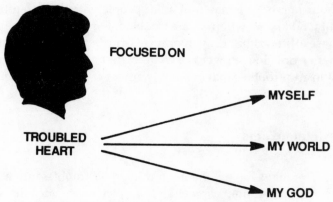

Fig. 7.1. Threefold Focus of a Troubled Heart

For this reason, he cries,

> Do not be far from me,
>   for trouble is near
>   and there is no one to help (v. 11).

We must be careful here. The Psalms never endorse a disrespectful anger or rebellion in prayer. On the contrary, the psalmists' devotion to God is evident in their constant appeal to Him for help in desperate situations. Every parent can spot a defiant, stubborn child who kicks and screams when he doesn't get his way. Yet, these same parents can also discern the cry of confusion and dismay that comes from a child seeking an answer in frustrating and perplexing circumstances. The same is true of God. He too knows when we are rebelling and when we are seeking His help in desperate situations. In this sense we are encouraged in Scripture to be open about our attitudes toward God. In addition to ourselves and the world around us, we may also communicate our questions and frustrations about God in our prayers (see fig. 7.1).

Unfortunately, however, Christians often try to hide their genuine attitudes from God. Sometimes, in everyday life, we work hard to conceal our heart's condition from our friends and neighbors. Even husbands and wives may refuse to reveal themselves to each other. Similarly, we often put on a happy face as we approach God in an attempt to cover up attitudes we deem inappropriate. Yet, God

knows our hearts. We may fool other people with smiles and flat-
tery, but God knows when we are troubled. For this reason, dealing
with these attitudes honestly in prayer is much better than trying to
hide them from God. Prayer is a channel for expressing to God the
confusion and troubles that inevitably enter every person's life.

Putting It Into Words

Many Christians have difficulty putting their troubles into words
when they pray. At home and church we pick up the idea that only
positive words are acceptable in prayer, so we never learn how to
express negative attitudes to God. Psalm 22 provides some guidelines that can help us to communicate effectively in this area.

Notice the distinctive manner in which the psalmist speaks of
himself. He does not simply say, "Lord, I am sad." Instead, he uses
a number of images to paint a vivid portrait of himself. He speaks of
himself as a worm (22:6). His condition is so bad that he can no
longer consider himself a man. He describes himself as melting wax
(22:14). His troubles have taken all his strength away. He sees
himself as a starving man (22:17). His plight has robbed him of all his
self-respect. Throughout the psalm, we find images drawn in dramatic and memorable detail.

In our prayers, we too can use vivid images and detailed descriptions of our condition. If we face rejection, we may feel like worthless rubbish. If this is how we feel, we should express that sentiment
in prayer. We should talk about our sense of uselessness. Christians
who suffer from loneliness can see themselves withering like thirst-
ing plants. They should communicate their intense longing for a
friend in dramatic terms. Prayer gives us the opportunity to tell God
what we think about ourselves. Stirring portraits of our lives can
help us lay our burdens at the feet of Christ and open ourselves
more fully to His comfort and healing.

The psalmist describes his trouble over outward circumstances in
the same way. He does not simply say, "Lord, things are pretty bad
down here." He talks about how he is mocked by others (22:7). He
even goes so far as to quote their mockery:

Fig. 7.2. Detailing Troubles in Prayer

> He trusts in the LORD;
>   let the LORD rescue him.
> Let him deliver him,
>   since he delights in him (22:8).

Then he uses the metaphors of bulls and lions to depict his ravaging enemies (22:12-13). He tells about their gambling over his clothing:

> They divide my garments among them
>   and cast lots for my clothing (22:18).

Note the detail with which the psalmist describes his circumstances. We too are invited to relate detailed and moving accounts of events in our lives. From small irritations to major crises, we may talk with God in detail about our circumstances.

   Observe the manner in which the psalmist expresses his attitudes toward God. He addresses God in a personal and intense way, calling Him "my God, my God" (22:1). Yet, he then calls attention to the ways in which God's actions seem out of accord with this personal relationship. He describes how God will not respond to his prayers, though he cries day and night (22:2). He points out the differences between God's present actions and His dealings with Israel in the past (22:4-5). He also contrasts his former relationship with God with his present condition (22:9-10). The psalmist's problem is one of confusion and frustration. God's actions seem to belie His divine nature and promises. Many times we face the same kinds of questions the psalmist faced. Through detailed depictions of God's dealings with us, we can open ourselves more fully to Him in our prayers (see fig. 7.2).

Every believer must find his or her own ways of communicating troubles in prayer. Different people express their attitudes differently. If our prayers are to be expressions of our hearts, they must bear the marks of our own personalities and interests. Nevertheless, the example of Psalm 22 demonstrates that the more detailed and dramatic we are, the more fully we communicate our troubles. Consequently, when we pray we must give careful attention to our laments about ourselves, our circumstances, and our God.

Limitations on Negatives

While honesty is essential to prayer, many portions of Scripture indicate that we must not go too far in expressing our negative feelings. Freedom without restraint in this area will inevitably lead to excess. Expressing our troubles to God can easily move into rebellion against Him. Therefore, we must heed Scripture's warnings about irreverent grumbling against God. Psalm 95:7b-9 solemnly warns us:

> Today, if you hear his voice,
>   do not harden your hearts as you did at Meribah,
>   as you did that day at Massah in the desert,
>   where your fathers tested and tried me,
>   though they had seen what I did.

The New Testament also exhorts us to avoid the example of Israel in the wilderness:

> And do not grumble, as some of them did—and were killed by the destroying angel (1 Cor. 10:10).

Both of these passages urge us not to imitate the rebellious grumbling of the Israelites.

By comparing the grumbling of the Israelites in Exodus and Numbers with Psalm 22, we can establish boundaries for our negative attitudes. Expressions of our troubles in prayer are subject to at least three limitations.

First, *we must maintain our fundamental trust in the goodness of God.*

The wandering Israelites questioned God's faithfulness in many of their complaints (e.g., Exod. 17:2, 7). They actually turned from faith to rebellion. By contrast, in Psalm 22, the psalmist never abandons his belief that God is trustworthy. He demonstrates loyalty to God by turning directly to Him for help. He trusts that somehow God remains personally concerned with him despite his difficult experiences. When we face situations that hide the faithfulness of God from our sight, we too should communicate our doubts and concerns to Him. In spite of our troubles, however, we must always remember that God is faithful. In such prayers, we are not questioning the reality of God's love. We are asking how particular events harmonize with His love. In this way, we may bring serious laments to God without denying His holiness and faithfulness. We talk honestly with God in the hope that He will once again make His goodness plain to us.

Second, *the expression of negative attitudes in prayer must not be motivated by greed or selfishness.* In the wilderness, the Israelites were not satisfied with God's provision of manna. They groaned at being denied the luxury of meat (Num. 11:4-35). This greed stands in sharp contrast to the attitude of Psalm 22. The psalmist approaches God with a genuine need, not with a desire for luxury. He is mocked, abused, and threatened. He is not demanding wealth or fame. His needs are genuine and his negative attitude stems from a desire for truth to prevail. As we bring our negative attitudes to God today, we must be careful to focus on our needs and not our selfish desires. Greed can be a rotting cancer in prayer. It can turn the plea of a humble child into the tantrum of a spoiled brat. We moan because we do not have a brand-new house. We complain because we do not have the expensive clothes we want. We grumble because we do not get to take that grand vacation. These can be wholesome pleasures to enjoy if they come our way in God's providence. Yet, we must not put God to the test by complaining about not having more when we already have so much. We must exclude selfish complaints from our prayers.

Third, *negative feelings must be accompanied by an openness to receiving God's response with gratitude.* In the wilderness, the Israelites often grumbled against a command from God (Num. 14:1-15). They were not ready to be instructed, corrected, or further enlightened on the

Fig. 7.3. Limitations on Negative Expressions

matters that concerned them. Psalm 22 displays the opposite attitude. The psalmist comes to God with questions and complaints but also with a readiness to listen and learn from God. After twenty-one verses of intense complaint and petition, his attitudes are transformed. He promises,

> I will declare your name to my brothers;
> in the congregation I will praise you (v. 22).

As we will see in a later chapter, this transformation probably resulted from a word of assurance coming to the psalmist through a priest, just as Eli assured Hannah (1 Sam. 1:17) and Jehaziel spoke to Jehoshaphat (2 Chron. 20:15-17). Whatever the case, the psalmist's words of praise show his willingness to have his attitude changed by God. He was not obstinate and rebellious. He sought God in his troubles and gladly received His blessing. Today we must avoid stubborn complaints. The Holy Spirit uses all kinds of things to confirm God's love for us. Reflection on Scripture, the encouragement of fellow believers, and our own inward wrestling with the issues help us to see that God still cares for us. Just as the psalmist, we must be ready to be taught by God. If we are open to the work of the Holy Spirit, we can gain new perspectives and outlooks on life through prayer, new insights that give us new attitudes. God invites us to express our negative feelings to Him, but we must also be ready to receive His help and provision (see fig. 7.3).

In this chapter, we have seen a vital dimension of communication with God. Prayer is a channel through which we may express our deepest troubles to Him in honesty and devotion. As we learn to do so, we will find that prayer can be a source of strength and encouragement in times of trouble.

Review Questions

1. Why do many Christians think prayer is improper if their attitudes are not entirely positive? What biblical evidence exists for expressing our troubled hearts in prayer? What three focal points can our troubles have?

2. What techniques did the psalmists use to communicate effectively the troubles they faced? How may we imitate these today?

3. What are three important limitations that must control us as we express our troubles in prayer? How do the stories of Israel's wilderness wanderings help us arrive at these limitations?

Exercises

1. List one thing that troubles you about yourself, your circumstances, and God. Using the criteria given in this chapter, describe how each of these negatives in your life can be a legitimate or illegitimate topic for prayer.

2. Choose a legitimate item mentioned in exercise 1 and describe your troubled attitude in three or four sentences. Be sure to use detailed and dramatic words that express your true attitude toward the item.

3. Write a six-to-eight-sentence prayer that focuses on a troubling

event most people know about (e.g., world hunger, war, economic troubles, sickness, etc.). As much as possible use the form below as a guide.

Holy Lord, You are _____
(description of God)

_____

_____. Yet, when we think of

_____
(a specific problem)

_____

_____, our hearts are

_____
(description of emotional reaction)

_____

_____.

We see _____
(sights of the event)

_____. We hear

_____
(sounds of the event)

_____. These things trouble

us because _____

_____.

In our helpless state we turn to You for _____

_____. Hear us, O Lord, and

come to our aid. Amen.

Extended Exercise

This week pray at least three times with the exclusive purpose of expressing to God how troubled you are about something in your life. Be sure to be honest and dramatic in your description of these matters. You may find the form in exercise 3 helpful.

8

In Times of Joy

Jesus, I am resting, resting
In the joy of what thou art;
I am finding out the greatness
Of thy loving heart.
                    Jean Sophia Pigott
                    1845-82

After several years of waiting, a young couple was about to adopt the child they had wanted for so long. Lengthy interviews and countless forms never dulled their enthusiasm. Great joy overflowed as they anticipated having a little one in their home. When the child finally arrived, everything seemed perfect. The baby cooed at just the right times. She smiled for the grandparents and neighbors. The young couple could not have been happier. But at two o'clock the next morning, trouble began. The baby cried and cried. The next night it was the same; she had to be held for the entire night. After a third sleepless night, the exhausted father said to his wife, "Honey, I thought this child was going to make us happy, but all she does is cause problems."

Experienced parents have mixed reactions to this story. They understand that parenting takes hard work and dedication, but they also wonder about this father's attitude. Does his child have to be perfect for him to take pleasure in the precious gift God has given him? Can he not marvel at his daughter, even though she puts heavy demands on him? Apparently this father lost sight of the beauty of his baby. The difficulties he faced robbed him of his joy.

We may jump to criticize this ungrateful father, but many of us have the same blurred vision in other areas of life. We too receive tremendous blessings but fail to delight fully in them because of problems that remain in our lives. We have a wonderful meal but complain about washing the dishes. We own a lovely home but moan about mowing the grass. We are blessed with healthy bodies but groan about the color of our hair. As a result, we should all take a good look at our attitudes. What joys may we expect to have as believers? How are we to make these attitudes a part of our prayers?

Two Kinds of Joy

When we speak of Christian joy, a variety of experiences comes to mind. First, we remember the times God has granted a quiet, peaceful joy to our hearts in the midst of trouble. Deep within our souls God has instilled a confidence that He will never leave us alone. Even when life presents hardships and troubles, we know that Christ is with us:

> And surely I will be with you always, to the very end of the age (Matt. 28:20b).

As the psalmist puts it,

> Even though I walk
> through the valley of the shadow of death,
> I will fear no evil,
> for you are with me;
> your rod and your staff,
> they comfort me (Ps. 23:4).

Though difficulties assail us on every side, they can never utterly destroy the possibility of inner peace through faith. Confidence in the power of God sustains us and makes us victors even in apparent defeat:

> Who shall separate us from the love of Christ? Shall trouble or hardship or persecution or famine or nakedness or danger or sword? As it is written:

"For your sake we face death all day long;
We are considered as sheep to be slaughtered."

No, in all these things we are more than conquerors through
him who loved us (Rom. 8:35-37).

Unbelievers often try to ignore the torments of life, but they
seldom overlook them forever. Eventually, many people without
faith in Christ collapse in despair for they have no basis for hope. By
contrast, Christians can survive these ordeals with the peace and joy
of knowing God's love. When little children become ill, they rest in
the arms of their loving parents. Gentle parental care soothes and
lifts their spirits. As children of God, we experience a similar comfort and peace, knowing that the arms of our heavenly Father are
around us. In this sense, Christian joy is a simple, quiet confidence
in the faithfulness of the Lord. We face struggles, but we take joy in
God's care for us.

Second, the wonder of being a child of God is not merely having
an inner peace during hardship. Sometimes God's blessings are so
extraordinary that we are overcome with excitement. Special events
come our way from time to time—the birth of a healthy child, the
sudden healing of a sick friend, a major accomplishment in life.
Acknowledging the wonder of these events overwhelms our hearts
with exuberant joy. In fact, the evils of life seem to vanish before our
eyes as we bathe in the splendor of the moment. As the dawning
sun chases the shadows of night far away, God's special blessings
can turn gloom into glorious delight.

This kind of joy is evident in the enthusiasm of the psalmist who
said:

Praise God in his sanctuary;
    praise him in his mighty heavens.
Praise him for his acts of power;
    praise him for his surpassing greatness.
Praise him with the sounding of the trumpet,
    praise him with the harp and lyre,
praise him with tambourine and dancing,
    praise him with the strings and flute,
praise him with the clash of cymbals,
    praise him with resounding cymbals.

Fig. 8.1. Christian Joy

Let everything that has breath praise the LORD (Ps. 150:1b-6a).

Consider the excitement expressed in this psalm. The psalmist does not mutter a simple "Thank you, Lord." He is so overcome with the goodness of God that he excitedly invites everyone to praise God. He begins by calling for the praise of God in heaven and earth. He announces the basis for praise in God's work and character. He even lists the many instruments of praise in the temple worship. Then he enthusiastically concludes,

Let everything that has breath praise the LORD (v. 6).

The picture painted in this passage is not that of a child peacefully resting in a parent's arms but of the child of God's jumping up and down, full of the joy and excitement of Christmas morning. The difficulties that certainly surround the psalmist are not even mentioned here. For the moment, they are forgotten. His troubles make room for a full enjoyment of God. In this sense, Christian joy can be an exuberant delight in God (see fig. 8.1).

Most believers can testify to experiencing a quiet joy in Christ from time to time, but a spirit of full celebration captures the hearts of believers less frequently. Daily life is mediocre at best for most Christians; often it is fairly miserable. Even when noteworthy blessings come, they see only the added responsibilities and troubles that are sure to follow. No matter what happens, they can take little delight in life.

I remember once hearing a minister who had this view. He told his congregation that Christians should never expect to be happier than unbelievers. As far as he was concerned, life in this world is simply miserable, and the sooner we admit it the better. Sadly, his message reflected the terrible condition of his own life more than the possibilities that Christ offers us. He was a troubled man, and his theology was unable to help him. He never hoped for a joyful life, and he never seemed to get it. So many Christians live all their lives closed to the joys God bestows.

Worse still, the absence of exuberant joy can eventually lead to an overriding pessimism. Pessimism then moves quickly into complacency about religious matters, which eventually produces complete apathy toward the cause of Christ. In this state, some downhearted believers even move toward total apostasy. The occasional experience of exuberant joy in Christ is not an optional luxury. It is a vital part of our Christian experience, for it strengthens us and keeps us pressing forward in the service of Christ.

Thus, we may speak of Christian joy in at least two senses: a quiet confidence in the care of Christ, and an exuberant rejoicing over His marvelous blessings. Both dimensions of joy are precious and indispensable to the Christian life.

A Way to Joy

Many barriers keep us from Christian joy. Traumatic disappointments separate us from full delight in the grace of God. Guilt over sin also dulls our appreciation of God's blessings. At times, life's troubles bring us so much misery that it seems we will be forever under their load. Although many Christian groups claim to have the secret for constant happiness, they offer solutions that are simplistic and shortsighted. Despite the sincerity of these attempts, they fail to yield the expected results. Life continues to hurl obstacles in our paths. Burdens are still placed on our shoulders. Struggles still confront us. We can be utterly free from hardship only if we completely cut ourselves off from reality. If this is our situation, how can we bring joy into our lives? Is there a path to joy?

The Psalms are filled with examples of believers who use prayer as a way to joy. As we saw in the previous chapter, the psalmists lament before God, but their frank displays of negative feelings often lead to the fresh discovery of joy. For instance, Psalm 59 begins deep in despair:

> See how they lie in wait for me!
>> Fierce men conspire against me
>> for no offense or sin of mine, O LORD.
> I have done no wrong, yet they are ready to attack me.
>> Arise to help me; look on my plight! (vv. 3,4).

Yet, a different attitude emerges toward the end:

> O my Strength, I sing praise to you;
>> you, O God, are my fortress, my loving God (v. 17).

Similarly, Psalm 13 also reveals a troubled spirit at first:

> How long must I wrestle with my thoughts
>> and every day have sorrow in my heart?
> How long will my enemy triumph over me? (v. 2).

But the same prayer ends with a joyful proclamation of praise:

> But I trust in your unfailing love;
>> my heart rejoices in your salvation.
> I will sing to the LORD,
>> for he has been good to me (vv. 5,6).

We find countless examples of this pattern among the Psalms.

Although most psalms of lament end with joy, one exception stands out boldly. Psalm 88 begins and ends on an entirely negative note. It begins with troubles:

> O LORD, the God who saves me,
>> day and night I cry out before you (v. 1).

And it ends in the same condition:

> You have taken my companions and loved ones from me;
>> the darkness is my closest friend (v. 18).

Psalm 88 shows us that prayer is not a magical joy pill. We must not think that talking with God will automatically bring an end to all of our sorrows. Some troubles stay with us for a long time. Even the apostle Paul had to learn to live with his "thorn in the flesh":

> Three times I pleaded with the Lord to take it away from me. But he said to me, "My grace is sufficient for you, for my power is made perfect in weakness" (2 Cor. 12:8-9).

Some forms of hardship remain with us even until death.

Nevertheless, the positive resolution of most psalms indicates clearly that prayer can be one effective way to discover joy. The examples of so many psalms teach us that joy is a goal for which we must strive in prayer. They assure us that prayer can indeed help us overcome the burden of our problems.

Psalm 73 recounts the experience of one psalmist. He tells of his search for understanding:

> For I envied the arrogant
>   when I saw the prosperity of the wicked.
>
> They have no struggles;
>   their bodies are healthy and strong.
> They are free from the burdens common to man;
>   they are not plagued by human ills.
> Therefore pride is their necklace;
>   they clothe themselves with violence.
> From their callous hearts comes iniquity;
>   the evil conceits of their minds know no limits.
> They scoff, and speak with malice;
>   in their arrogance they threaten oppression.
> Their mouths lay claim to heaven,
>   and their tongues take possession of the earth.
> Therefore their people turn to them
>   and drink up waters in abundance.
> They say, "How can God know?
>   Does the Most High have knowledge?" (vv. 3-11).

As far as the psalmist can tell, unbelievers live in their sins but suffer no sign of trouble. As he puts it,

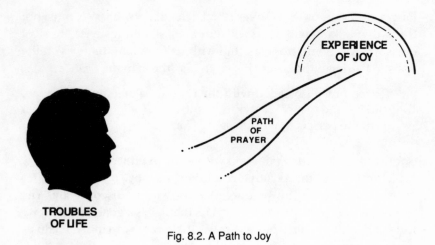

Fig. 8.2. A Path to Joy

This is what the wicked are like—
    always carefree, they increase in wealth (v. 12).

This observation frustrates him:

When I tried to understand all this,
    it was oppressive to me (v. 16).

Yet, he also tells how he found a resolution to his trouble:

. . . I entered the sanctuary of God;
    then I understood their final destiny (v. 17).

The psalmist did not attempt to solve this problem on his own. Nor did he merely discuss the matter with his friends as we often do. Instead, he went to God to resolve his questions. He entered the sanctuary, prayed, and found his answer. In worship and prayer his eyes were opened to reality. God reminded him of the ultimate destiny of the wicked and his troubled heart was relieved.

Even today, we must search for joy through prayer. Paul says to the Philippians:

Rejoice in the Lord always. I will say it again: Rejoice! (Phil. 4:4).

But notice how he tells them to find this attitude of rejoicing:

> Do not be anxious about anything, but in everything, by prayer and petition, with thanksgiving, present your requests to God. And the peace of God, which transcends all understanding, will guard your hearts and your minds in Christ Jesus (Phil. 4:6-7).

When we are anxious or troubled, we must seek God and cast our cares at His feet. As we pray with our hearts focused on God's Word and sensitive to the inward ministry of His Spirit, prayer can become a wonderful path to joy (see fig. 8.2).

The Expression of Joy

Prayer is not only a path to joy; it is also an opportunity to express joy. We find both quiet and exuberant gladness in biblical prayers. Just as troubles occupy a prominent place in many psalms, so expressions of happiness appear in many places. Unfortunately, however, the prayers of many believers today do not emphasize joy. Whole groups can pray for long periods with little sense of happiness. At best, we casually express our thanksgiving in a sentence or two. Yet, even these efforts are often so restrained that they hardly compare to the examples of rejoicing in the Bible.

One reason we neglect this dimension of prayer is our preoccupation with sorrows and needs when we talk with God. For a short while I served as a hospital chaplain intern. One of my responsibilities was to frequent the chapel of the hospital to offer help to those who were there. It was not unusual to find people in the chapel asking God to heal a loved one. If the situation was desperate enough, they would spend hours there. Nevertheless, not one time did I find someone in the chapel expressing joy before God for a patient's recovery. When a sick friend gets well, we simply say, "Praise the Lord," and return to our daily business. The sad fact is that we put a higher priority on our needs than on celebration in prayer. As important as our petitions may be, however, we must be careful not to allow them to crowd out joy in prayer.

When we talk with God about His blessings, our prayers can be filled with both quiet and exuberant joy. On the one hand, quiet peace can be a vital part of our prayers. The psalmist expresses this attitude in Psalm 131:

> My heart is not proud, O LORD,
>   my eyes are not haughty;
> I do not concern myself with great matters
>   or things too wonderful for me.
> But I have stilled and quieted my soul;
>   like a weaned child with its mother,
>   like a weaned child is my soul within me.
>
> O Israel, put your hope in the LORD
>   both now and forevermore.

In appreciation for the goodness that God has shown him, the psalmist tells the Lord about his humble and trusting spirit. Notice the careful contemplation of this attitude within the psalm. The psalmist does not pass over it quickly. He paints a captivating picture of his inner peace. As a weaned child rests quietly at his mother's breast, the psalmist rests in the arms of God. At this moment, he is not asking anything of God. Instead, he relaxes, delighted in knowing the love of his Creator and Savior.

In a similar way, we too can express our awareness of peace in Christ. We may wish to describe how an event reminds us of God's loving care. We may express an intuitive sense of the warmth and safety God gives us in a cold and threatening world. Whatever the case, we will benefit greatly from focusing on the details of these matters. Just as parents delight in hearing words of love from their children, God enjoys hearing us talk about the quiet joy we have in Him.

On the other hand, we may also express exuberant joy in prayer. The Psalms display this type of rejoicing in many ways. Musical instruments are called into service. The people are invited to sing, shout, clap, and dance. Enthusiasm is evident in all of these acts of celebration. As Psalm 9:1a puts it,

> I will praise you, O LORD, with all my heart.

All too often Christians relate their positive attitudes in a dull monotone. But consider how excited we become when we are happy in other circumstances. A new father tells his friends about his baby with the enthusiasm of his whole heart in his voice. Victorious athletes leave the playing field, hands lifted and hearts exhilarated with the thrill of winning. And yet, we are seldom comfortable expressing the same excitement over religious matters. We are accustomed to enthusiasm in ordinary contexts, but we often shrink from strong, positive feelings about matters related to Christ. If we become so exuberant about the ordinary affairs of life, how much more enthusiastic should we be in expressing our joys to God!

Enthusiastic joy in prayer raises an important question. What experiences bring us this kind of exhilaration? The psalmists find their delight in God, the creation around them, and their personal lives. *First*, joy rises out of reflection on God. His splendor is the concern of one passage:

> Praise the LORD, O my soul.
>
> O LORD my God, you are very great;
>   you are clothed with splendor and majesty (Ps. 104:1).

His mercy is the focus of another psalm:

> Praise the LORD, all you nations;
>   extol him, all you peoples.
> For great is his love toward us,
>   and the faithfulness of the LORD endures forever.
>
> Praise the LORD (Ps. 117).

Thinking about how wonderful God is often fills us with great happiness, for this is the God who has set His redemptive love on us.

Second, the psalmists look at the world around them and see God's blessings there. Many circumstances and events also create an overwhelming joy in the hearts of the faithful. In Psalm 104:24-25 we read:

> How many are your works, O LORD!
>   In wisdom you made them all;
>   the earth is full of your creatures.

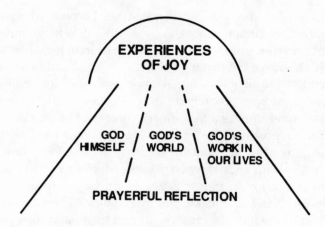

Fig. 8.3. Sources of Joy in Prayer

> There is the sea, vast and spacious,
>   teeming with creatures beyond number—
>   living things both large and small.

Reflection on God's providential care over the world also creates excitement and happiness in prayer.

Third, the psalmists express joy by enumerating the ways God has blessed their personal lives. One psalmist notes:

> How can I repay the LORD
>   for all his goodness to me?
> I will lift up the cup of salvation
>   and call on the name of the LORD.
> I will fulfill my vows to the LORD
>   in the presence of all his people (Ps. 116:12-14).

Exuberant Christian joy comes as we consider God's blessing in our personal lives as well. His care over every detail of our individual needs and concerns can delight our hearts.

Prayer is an opportunity for us to tell God about our joys. We are called upon to display our happiness in Him. Talking about the wonders of God, the world around us, and our personal lives gives us the opportunity to express excitement and joy in prayer (see fig. 8.3).

In this chapter we have focused on joy in prayer. Quiet and exuberant joy are essential parts of our Christian experience. Prayer relates to these positive attitudes in two ways. On the one hand, it can be an avenue for discovering joy in this troubled life. On the other hand, it can be an opportunity for celebrating our happiness in Christ. In these ways, joy in prayer may be a rewarding dimension of every Christian's life.

Review Questions

1. In what two senses may we speak of Christian joy? Why is the lack of joy harmful to a Christian?

2. In what ways can prayer be a means to joy? How may we transform trouble into joy as we pray? Should we always expect to discover joy in prayer?

3. Why do Christians often fail to make rejoicing an important part of their prayers? How do biblical examples demonstrate celebration in prayer?

Exercises

1. Name two blessings from God that have brought you a quiet joy from time to time. Identify two blessings from God that have overwhelmed you with exuberant joy at some time.

2. Consider one of the blessings that has led you to exuberant joy. Describe in detail how God gave you this blessing. Also describe how it made you feel and why.

3. Write a six-to-eight-sentence prayer focusing on a grand event that most Christians consider important (e.g., the birth of Christ, the resurrection, the provision of food, etc.). As much as possible, use the following form as a guide.

Blessed God, You are _____
                                                (description)

_____ .

We celebrate before You, for You have worked wonders. We think

of _____
                          (Choose a blessing.)

_____ ,

and our hearts are _____
                                    (Describe an emotional reaction.)

_____ .

We remember _____
                              (Describe the details of the blessing.)

_____ .

These things make us _____ ,
                                      (Describe an emotion.)

and we rejoice before You. Blessed are You, O Lord. Amen.

Extended Exercise

At least three times this week, pray expressing joy for blessings the
Lord has bestowed upon you. You may wish to follow the form
given in exercise 3.

9

In Times of Need

I need thee, O I need thee,
Every hour I need thee;
O bless me now, my Saviour,
I come to thee.
                    Robert Lowry
                    1826-99

As a young child I suffered from asthma. Most of the time I enjoyed running and playing just like other children, never giving my health a second thought. But occasionally, when I least expected it, I would suddenly be unable to catch my breath. For hours, under the duress of wheezing and coughing, I struggled for air. Every ounce of energy was spent gasping for enough to stay alive.

Many such incidents in our lives make us dramatically aware of our needs. Sometimes our needs are major; at other times they are relatively small. Hardly a moment goes by when we do not sense some kind of need, whether weighty or trivial. It is not surprising, therefore, that petitions occupy a prominent place in our communication with God. For this reason, we must look carefully at our attitudes. What motives should lie behind our petitions? What are we trying to change when we ask God for things? How may we expect God to respond to our requests?

Need and Greed

"Can't you ever be satisfied?" a friend asks his disgruntled neighbor. "You always want more, more, more. I think it's about time you begin to realize how good you have it." These words sound familiar to many of us. If we haven't heard them directed at us, then we have thought them about someone else. It is a common human problem; we find it hard to be satisfied with what we have. We drive around town and say to ourselves, "I wish I had a car like that one." Or, "It would be so nice to have a house that big." Especially in the affluent cultures of the world, we are always striving for more and more.

The generation now embarking on adulthood has been called the "me" generation, and in many ways the description is accurate. Since sin came into the world, humans have always had trouble with selfishness. In recent years, however, greed has spread like cancer to nearly every conceivable part of our lives. We are so concerned with our own well-being that we have become consumed with ourselves. "What's good for me is what's good!"

Sadly, this principle has also taken hold of our prayers. We often turn to God with grossly selfish requests. In light of God's many gifts to us, our prayers must often sound to Him like an ungrateful child whining in a toy store. "Will you buy this for me? Will you buy this for me, too? This too? Why not?" After God has given so much, we always come back asking for more.

To avoid this pitfall, we must examine our motives as we make our requests to God. The Bible tells us repeatedly that it is good to request what we need. As Jesus put it,

> Give us today our daily bread (Matt. 6:11).

However, we are not free to ask from selfish motives. James emphatically forbids us to make requests out of greed:

> When you ask, you do not receive, because you ask with wrong motives, that you may spend what you get on your pleasures (James 4:3).

We may bring all sorts of legitimate needs to God, but self-centered requests must be excluded from prayer. As we examine our attitudes, we must be sure that our petitions stem more from need and less from greed.

One helpful way to guard against greed in prayer is to couch petitions in a deep and abiding sense of contentment with God's provisions. Contentment extinguishes greed as water douses a blazing fire. Paul addresses this matter in no uncertain terms:

> But godliness with contentment is great gain. For we brought nothing into the world, and we can take nothing out of it. But if we have food and clothing, we will be content with that. People who want to get rich fall into temptation and a trap and into harmful desires that plunge men into ruin and destruction. For the love of money is a root of all kinds of evil. Some people, eager for money, have wandered from the faith and pierced themselves with many griefs (1 Tim. 6:6-10).

In these verses, contentment is set in sharp contrast to a compulsive desire for the things of the world. People who know contentment are basically appreciative of what they have while others are driven by a destructive desire for more and more. On a day to day basis, Christians must strive not only to focus on what they desire, but also to see the many good things God has already provided. When we spend time in prayer talking about the blessings God has already given, we go a long way toward avoiding self-centered petitioning. Paul encouraged the early church about this:

> Do not be anxious about anything, but in everything, by prayer and petition, with thanksgiving, present your requests to God (Phil. 4:6).

Paul is not teaching here that we must simply say "Thank you" before asking for something. His insight goes much deeper than this. Instead, he reminds us that God has already given us a rich bounty. As we recall this goodness, we will be better able to distinguish requests of need from those of greed (see fig. 9.1).

Seeking Change

Whenever we ask God to grant something we need, we are asking Him in effect to direct the events of the world. In one way or another this motivation raises several important questions about our petitions. Do we try to change God through prayer? Are our requests

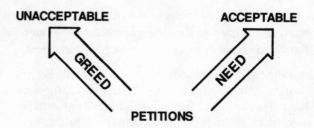

Fig. 9.1. Motives and Petitions

intended to compel Him to act in ways He did not already intend? If God is unchanging, why do we bother to pray at all?

To answer these questions, we must look at prayer from two vantage points. In one sense petitions certainly do not change God. In another sense, however, prayers are ordained by God Himself as a means of moving Him to action. Unfortunately, many Christian groups tend to emphasize one of these viewpoints to the near exclusion of the other.

On the one hand, Scripture clearly teaches that God has a comprehensive and unchangeable plan for His creation. His designs for history have been set and cannot be altered. In Ephesians 1:11 we read that God has a purpose that extends to all creation:

> In him we were also chosen, having been predestined according to the plan of him who works out everything in conformity with the purpose of his will.

Similarly, Proverbs 16:4 says that God sovereignly ordains a purpose for every event in history:

> The LORD works out everything for his own ends—
>   even the wicked for a day of disaster.

Beyond this, God has not only set a course for the world, but has done so immutably. In Isaiah 46:9-10 we read:

> Remember the former things, those of long ago;
>   I am God, and there is no other;
>   I am God, and there is none like me.
> I make known the end from the beginning,

from ancient times, what is still to come.
I say: My purpose will stand,
and I will do all that I please.

The plans and purposes of God are not subject to approval. What He decrees will stand firm:

But he stands alone, and who can oppose him?
He does whatever he pleases.
He carries out his decree against me,
and many such plans he still has in store (Job 23:13-14).

In this ultimate sense, therefore, it is folly to think that prayer changes God. Trying to alter the eternal decrees of God through prayer is like trying to reach the moon on a trampoline; it is impossible. Our petitions cannot interrupt God's plan for the universe any more than a trampoline can break the power of earth's gravity. This fact should comfort us greatly. The Lord's decrees reflect His wisdom and goodness. When evil wreaks havoc in our lives, we can take solace in the knowledge that our holy God has ordained the events of history. As the Lord of creation, God is able to take evil in this life and transform it into good:

And we know that in all things God works for the good of those who love him, who have been called according to his purpose (Rom. 8:28).

Thankfully, nothing can thwart God's sovereignty over His world. In this sense, therefore, it is impossible for prayer to change God.

On the other hand, however, Scripture teaches that prayer has been ordained as a way by which God may be moved to action. We must be careful to understand this dimension of prayer correctly. In the first place, God's plan is so comprehensive that it not only includes the final destinies of things but also includes the secondary, creaturely processes that work together to accomplish these ends. For instance, God does not simply ordain light to shine on the earth each day; He also employs the sun, the moon, the stars, and countless other things to accomplish that end. God does not merely determine that someone will recover from a disease; He uses doctors and medicine to accomplish the healing. As the playwright of his-

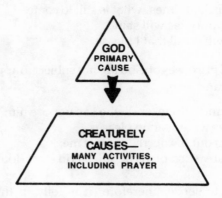

Fig. 9.2. Prayer as a Cause of Change

tory, God did not simply write an ending for the book of time. He wrote every word on every page so that all events lead to the grand finale.

Furthermore, on those pages of history, God wrote a part for Himself. God is dramatically involved in the course of the world. He delights in personally directing and guiding events. He does not sit back and watch the world go its own way; He involves Himself with creatures one way at this moment and another way at that moment. He allows certain patterns to develop for a time and then reverses those patterns to accomplish another end. From a divine perspective, God's plan is clear and sure, even though His plan unfolds in ways that cannot be fully understood from a limited human perspective.

But still the inevitable question arises. Why pray when God already knows and controls everything? The same question may be asked of other areas of life. Why go to the doctor? Why work a job? Why spread the gospel? The reason we do all these things is that God has established these actions as vital creaturely means for accomplishing His purposes. The same is also true of prayer. Prayer is one of the many secondary causes through which God fulfills His plan.

Unfortunately, however, many Christians treat prayer as an impotent human activity. "If you want something done," we tend to think, "stop praying and go do it." To be sure, prayer and action must be kept in balance, but we must stop viewing prayer as so much wishful thinking. Communication with God is our way of tapping into the power of the Lord of the universe. It is something we can use to move history toward its end more effectively and dramatically than any other human effort. In His sovereignty, God has made prayer a wonderfully powerful means by which we may interact with Him and effectively shape the course of history. When we petition God, we approach Him on the plane of His involvement with secondary causes. We seek to change the world by calling on the One who actively orders the world day by day (see fig. 9.2).

In the exodus from Egypt, Moses once faced a desperate situation. The people had rebelled against God and stirred His anger to such an extent that He was going to destroy the nation of Israel:

> "I have seen these people," the LORD said to Moses, "and they are a stiff-necked people. Now leave me alone so that my anger may burn against them and that I may destroy them. Then I will make you into a great nation" (Exod. 32:9-10).

Had any one of us been in Moses' shoes, we would probably have stepped aside. "After all," we would have thought, "how can prayer change this situation?" But Moses had great faith and courage. He lifted his heart in prayer and attempted to dissuade God from His destructive intentions:

> But Moses sought the favor of the LORD his God. "O LORD," he said, "why should your anger burn against your people, whom you brought out of Egypt with great power and a mighty hand? Why should the Egyptians say, 'It was with evil intent that he brought them out, to kill them in the mountains and to wipe them off the face of the earth'? Turn from your fierce anger; relent and do not bring disaster on your people. Remember your servants Abraham, Isaac and Israel, to whom you swore by your own self: 'I will make your descendants as numerous as the stars in the sky and I will give your descendants all this land I promised them, and it will be their inheritance forever'" (Exod. 32:11-13).

In response to the prayer of His servant, God turned back and had mercy on the people:

Then the LORD relented and did not bring on his people the disaster he had threatened (Exod. 32:14).

We must remember that Moses did not alter the eternal decrees of God; his prayer did not take God by surprise, nor did it force God into doing something He had not planned. Yet, this text illustrates that God uses prayer as an effective means of fulfilling His purposes. He has chosen to use the petitions of His people as instruments of change. Prayer is a powerul human effort that can significantly affect not only the lives of individuals but the very course of world history.

Expectations and Resignation

What kinds of expectations may we have when we make requests of God? Will He give us what we want or not? Christians disagree on this subject. Some believers argue, "God wants you to have everything you desire! Just believe with your whole heart as you pray, and God will shower His blessings on you." But other Christians demand, "Trust in the will of God. Pray not for your will but for God's will, and trust Him to do the right thing."

Torn by these different views, Christians are often confused about what to do. Should we expect God to answer our prayers or should we resign ourselves to whatever happens? As we shall see, valid arguments exist on both sides of this controversy. Each perspective captures a dimension of the biblical picture. Nevertheless, both points of view also have serious flaws.

On the one hand, we must always remember that faith requires a humble trust in God.

> God opposes the proud
> but gives grace to the humble (James 4:6).

Forsaking our own plans and accepting the holy plan of God is an essential ingredient in serving Christ. Resisting God leads to destruction, but trusting in Him brings eternal life. As the proverb says,

Trust in the LORD with all your heart
   and lean not on your own understanding;
in all your ways acknowledge him,
   and he will make your paths straight (Prov. 3:5,6).

Little children sometimes advise their parents on how to drive the family car. "Why don't you turn here, Daddy?" "Park the car over there, Mom." Normally, we chuckle quietly, knowing that children have little idea of the best choices in these matters. They would be better off trusting their parents' judgment. Similarly, we should be ready to resign ourselves to God's will for His wisdom goes far beyond our human insight. Our own hopes and plans often lead us into great disappointment and trouble, but the designs of God are firm and sure.

In this light, we should not be surprised that Jesus taught His disciples to pray,

Your kingdom come,
Your will be done
   on earth as it is in heaven (Matt. 6:10).

Our deepest desire should be to see the will of God realized in the affairs of humanity as it is in the perfection of heaven. The example of Jesus' prayer in the Garden of Gethsemane is also instructive:

He went away a second time and prayed, "My Father, if it is not possible for this cup to be taken away unless I drink it, may your will be done" (Matt. 26:42).

Jesus knew that the plan of God included His death and resurrection. He had foretold it many times during His lifetime. Consequently, even though His personal desire was in some measure to the contrary, Jesus resigned Himself to do the will of the Father. As followers of Christ, we too must be ready to submit our personal desires to the plans of God.

Nevertheless, serious dangers lurk behind an attitude of total resignation. Trust in God's providence can easily turn into passive fatalism. If we continually focus on how our circumstances are blessed by the hand of divine providence, before long we will see little reason to petition God. Such was the reasoning of the child who prayed at bedtime, "God, You already know everything. So, I don't need to ask You to take care of it. Amen." In effect, adults often pray in a similar way. When someone becomes ill, we simply commit the matter to God's will rather than seek to change the situation through prayer. When a family falls apart, we throw up our hands at what appears to be inevitable, instead of asking God to remedy the hurt and pain.

Despite the apparent piety of such resignation, these attitudes are often evidence of fatalism, not faith. As a fatalistic attitude grows within us, prayer becomes less and less important. Placing too high a premium on resignation can seriously hinder our prayers. Why ask for things to be different if the best is already ours? We must be careful, therefore, not to allow a wholesome trust in God's providence to lead us away from enthusiastic involvement in prayer.

Contrary to an extreme attitude of total resignation, Jesus taught that prayer involves expectation as well:

> And I will do whatever you ask in my name, so that the Son may bring glory to the Father. You may ask me for anything in my name, and I will do it (John 14:13-14).

Similarly, in John 16:23 we read:

> In that day you will no longer ask me anything. I tell you the truth, my Father will give you whatever you ask in my name.

Unhappily, believers frequently misunderstand these and similar passages (see also James 1:5; 1 John 3:22). Many Christians think that merely repeating the formula, "In Jesus' name," can insure that God will grant their requests. They refuse medical treatment because they have prayed in the name of Jesus. They make hasty financial commitments because they expect God to respond favorably to their prayers. Yet, in the contexts of these verses, Jesus makes it clear that prayer in His name is more than repeating a formula. It involves a wholehearted communion with Him in which the believer is conformed to Christ and His purposes:

> If you remain in me and my words remain in you, ask whatever you wish, and it will be given you (John 15:7).

To pray in Jesus' name is to pray in harmony with Him, seeking His intercession and submitting to Him as Lord. Christ does not assure us that all of our requests will be granted if we repeat a formula. Instead, He teaches that those requests which are in accordance with His name—that is, His holy character as our intercessor—will be granted by the Father.

Despite our good motives and high hopes, much of what we pray for simply does not materialize. We may want career advancements; we may need relief from personal problems; we may seek to be healed of afflictions. We may even believe with all our hearts that God will grant these requests. Nevertheless, sometimes these hopes are not fulfilled. God chooses to say no. How can we avoid severe disappointment in these situations? What expectations can we have as we pray? Should we have confidence in petitioning God?

Expectation in prayer operates on two basic levels. First, we must always maintain a general confidence in the goodness of God. No evil can be found in Him. In His purity, He delights only in doing good. As the psalmist put it,

> Taste and see that the LORD is good:
> blessed is the man who takes refuge in him (Ps. 34:8).

Moreover, Scripture tells us that God shows special goodness to His people in particular:

> Surely God is good to Israel,
> to those who are pure in heart (Ps. 73:1).

God's character lays an important foundation for expectations in prayer. Since God is good, we can always expect His responses to be good.

Often the Scriptures make specific petitions on the basis of God's goodness. For instance, in Psalm 25:7 we read,

> Remember not the sins of my youth
> and my rebellious ways;
> according to your love remember me,
> for you are good, O LORD.

Jesus drew upon this theme in a powerful manner as He taught on prayer:

> Ask and it will be given to you; seek and you will find; knock and the door will be opened to you. For everyone who asks receives; he who seeks finds; and to him who knocks, the door will be opened.
>   Which of you, if his son asks for bread, will give him a stone? Or if he asks for a fish, will give him a snake? If you, then, though you are evil, know how to give good gifts to your children, how much more will your Father in heaven give good gifts to those who ask him! (Matt. 7:7-11).

If human fathers can be relied upon to give good gifts to their children, how much more can we trust our heavenly Father to do the same? Decent human parents will never refuse to do good for their children if it is within their reach. All things are within the reach of God, and He will do only good for His children. As James put it,

> Every good and perfect gift is from above, coming down from the Father of the heavenly lights, who does not change like shifting shadows (James 1:17).

With this assurance in mind, we can bring our requests to God with a great deal of confidence. We do not need to fear that He will grant us stones when we ask for bread. He will not deceive us or lead us into evil. We can always count on Him to respond to our petitions with goodness.

However, a word of caution must be added. To affirm that God always does good is not to say that all of God's responses will seem good to us. Often the perfect actions of God can appear to be less than good from a human point of view. A family may pray for the healing of a loved one but never see a recovery. A Christian group may pray for a strong leader and find later that their leader is less than they expected. A nation may pray for peace and still be thrown into war. Cases like these can be perplexing. "We asked for something good. Why didn't God give it to us?"

In these situations, we must recognize that human limitations and biases can so skew our perception that we may not see reality as it actually is. I know a family that wanted to live in a particular neighborhood and was disappointed at first that God granted them a home elsewhere. After a few years, however, they realized the house they originally desired was a poor choice. Many times we can see God's goodness very easily. Other times we must wait a long time to see what holy purpose God had in responding to our prayers as He did. In fact, we will have to wait until we meet Him face to face to appreciate the wisdom of some of His ways. We may rest assured, however, that in one way or another God will always respond to our prayers with goodness.

Beyond this, confidence in prayer can also take the form of compelling certainty that particular things will be granted. At one time or another, most Christians have gone through this sort of experience. A feeling of certainty can come to us in many ways. Sometimes a promise of God in the Bible seems to fit perfectly with our need; this encourages us to believe that God will grant our request. In other situations, our confidence may be based on an analysis of the world around us. We conclude that God will grant us certain requests because the result will be so positive. At other times, we may simply sense intuitively that God will respond favorably to our request. Deep within our hearts, the Holy Spirit may convict us to expect God to act in certain ways. Any one or some combination of these factors will occasionally raise high expectations within us as we make specific requests of God.

We can find ample support in the Bible for the legitimacy of this kind of expectation. Throughout the Psalms we find that the psalmists went before God with a firm conviction that He would answer their prayers. In Psalm 17:6 we read,

> I call on you, O God, for you will answer me;
>   give ear to me and hear my prayer.

The psalmist is confident deep within his heart that God will listen to his request and answer him. Similarly, Psalm 38:15 again expresses confidence:

> I wait for you, O LORD;
>   you will answer, O Lord my God.

In Psalm 27 the psalmist faces the problem of rejection and mistreatment. In verse 10, however, he declares,

> Though my father and mother forsake me,
>   the LORD will receive me.

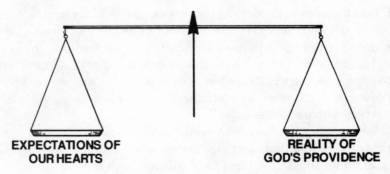

EXPECTATIONS OF   **REALITY OF**
OUR HEARTS   **GOD'S PROVIDENCE**

Fig. 9.3. Balanced Hopes in Prayer

These examples represent only a few of the specific expectations found again and again in the Psalms. From such texts we can see that, at times, believers may be deeply confident that God will answer their prayers.

As wonderful as these experiences seem, they can lead to two significant problems. First, some Christians treat prayer more like magic than communication with a divine Person. Magic assumes that correct formulas and strong belief will compel the powers of the universe to act in accordance with human wishes. Similarly, many Christians believe that their fervent belief can control the actions of God. Nothing could be further from the truth. Scripture makes it clear that God is free to do exactly as He pleases:

> Our God is in heaven;
> he does whatever pleases him (Ps. 115:3).

Prayer has no magical power to force God to fulfill His Word exactly as we expect. On the contrary, throughout history God has demonstrated His freedom to act in unexpected ways. As we pray we must always be sure to respect God's freedom.

A second problem stems from too much self-confidence. We often presume that our understanding of the Bible and of the world around us and our intuitive convictions are correct when they may not be. Although we may expect God to act in certain ways, we must be willing to adjust our evaluation in light of the ways He actually does act. Similarly, we must also be ready to question the inward convictions that come over us. They may be of the Holy Spirit, *or* they may in fact be merely our own desires. In other words, we must balance expectations with reality. If the acts of God do not follow what we expect, the difficulty lies not in God's integrity, but in the reliability of our judgments (see fig. 9.3).

Prayer has been given to us as a way of communicating attitudes of need to God. When we approach God with requests, we must avoid selfish greed. We must also come to God with the desire to see the world changed through prayer. Moreover, prayer is a time when we should balance our resignation to God's will with humble expectations resting on His goodness. In all these ways, prayer can be an effective way of bringing our needs to God.

Discussion Questions

1. In what ways can prayer stem from greed? How can we avoid selfish prayers?

2. If God's sovereign plan does not change, why do we pray? Does God really answer prayer?

3. How do Christians need to balance resignation and expectation in prayer? What general and particular expectations may we have as we make requests of God?

Exercises

1. List three desires of your heart that stem from need and three that stem from greed. What are the differences?

2. Give an example of something you expected God to give you but He did not. What divine wisdom can you hope to discern in His withholding that request?

3. Write a four-or-five-sentence prayer focusing on one need (not greed) and your expectations. As much as possible use the form below.

O God, _____
                              (description of God)

_____ .

I come to You not with greed but with sinceer need. Pleas grant

_____
                        (Describe the request.)

_____

_____ .

  I have confidence in Your goodness and hope for this blessing

because _____
              (Express a basis for confidence from the Bible, the world, or your own heart.)

_____

_____

_____ .

Please grant this request for Your glory. Amen.

Extended Exercise

Three times this week appeal to God to change something to which
you have been prone to resign yourself. Talk with Him in a realistic
manner about what hopes you have that He will answer.

Part Three

LOOKING AT
OUR COMMUNICATION

10

Form and Freedom in Prayer

Teach me, my God and King,
In all things thee to see,
And what I do in anything,
To do it as for thee.
George Herbert
1593-1632

In the preceding chapters, we examined the first two elements in our definition of prayer: God and the believer. We discovered that an awareness of God and of ourselves is crucial to fruitful prayer. At this point, a third dimension of prayer must be explored: prayer requires that we learn how to express ourselves. In the chapters that follow, we will consider this facet by asking such questions as, "How are we to talk effectively with God?" "Are there ways to communicate more fully our thoughts and attitudes to Him?"

One of the most basic elements of good communication in prayer is a proper balance between form and freedom. Unfortunately, defining what constitutes a proper balance stirs up heated controversy among believers. "I think it's insincere to stand up there and read a prayer," says one Christian. "Prayer is supposed to come from the heart, not from a piece of paper." But another believer counters, "When I take the time to plan my prayers, they are so much better than your senseless rambling."

This sort of controversy raises an important issue. How much forethought should we give to the content and arrangement of our prayers? Should we simply say what comes to mind, or should we

plan what we are going to say? Answers to these questions will vary
to some degree among different people and situations, but one
principle is applicable to all of us: going to extremes on either side of
this issue will severely hinder our prayers. We must search for ways
to balance form and freedom in our communication with God.

Freedom in Prayer

Many Christians emphasize the value of freedom in prayer. Although they usually find general guidelines helpful, these believers
want to avoid formulas and preconceived patterns as much as
possible. They give spontaneity and informality high priority when
talking with God. This view has much to its credit.

In the first place, God has revealed Himself to us in ways that
invite us to speak with Him on an informal level. Often the Bible
portrays God as our Father. This portrait was crucial to Jesus' model
prayer:

> Our Father in heaven,
> hallowed be your name (Matt. 6:9).

Although the title "Father" implies authority, power, and respect, it
also speaks of God's personal attention to us as His children. As
Paul put it,

> Because you are sons, God sent the Spirit of his Son into our
> hearts, the Spirit who calls out, "Abba, Father" (Gal. 4:6).

Beyond this, the Scriptures also teach that God is our friend. James
describes Abraham, saying,

> "Abraham believed God, and it was credited to him as right-
> eousness," and he was called God's *friend* (James 2:23).

Christ's incarnation is the most dramatic demonstration that God
desires to be close to His people. In this vein, Jesus Himself said:

> I no longer call you servants, because a servant does not know
> his master's business. Instead, I have called you *friends*, for

everything that I learned from my Father I have made known to you (John 15:15).

Since God has revealed an intimate concern for us, it is appropriate at times for us to talk with Him in an informal, spontaneous manner.

On occasion, children will take the time to think through what they want to say to their parents. They may even go to their rooms and rehearse unusual requests or important announcements. Report cards, for example, are often given to parents with carefully planned introductions and excuses. While this may be the case at special times, it is not generally the practice of healthy homes. When love and affection are strong in a family, children feel free to talk spontaneously with Mom and Dad.

In a similar way, we have also been given much freedom in our communication with God. Our heavenly Father has shown us intimate love beyond measure. Because of this relationship we may speak with Him freely and informally. The formality of a planned speech is not necessary when we talk with one so close to us. Our intimacy with God forms a solid basis for freedom in prayer.

Beyond this, not only are informal prayers based on our intimacy with God, they also enhance our personal relationship with Him. All too often the formal language of traditional prayers places a barrier between Christians and God. Using "thees" and "thous" or reciting memorized prayers can prevent genuine communication. The heavy ball and chain of formalism can make it difficult for some to experience a vibrant relationship with God.

Happily, however, we can loosen these weights and enjoy a fresh awareness of God through more spontaneity in prayer. Several Christians I know were brought up in formal, liturgical churches. Through constant exposure, they lost sight of the many benefits offered by their traditional style of worship. In college, they began to attend a church that was very informal. As you might expect, they discovered a heightened sense of joy in worship and prayer at their new church. Informal, conversational prayer soon became one of their favorite Christian activities. For many people, a constant diet of formality can be spiritual poison. In such cases, informality can

	PSALM 4	PSALM 5
INVOCATION	1	1-3
LAMENT	2-6a	4-7
PETITION	6b	8-10
CONFIDENCE	7-8	11-12

Fig. 10.1. Common Elements of Laments

revive our souls and make us powerfully aware of God as a Father and friend.

However, while informality has many advantages, it can also create serious problems. Two difficulties are particularly common. First, an emphasis on freedom sometimes leads inadvertently to its own kind of dead formalism. When we pay little conscious attention to the content of our prayers, they tend to become rote and repetitious simply by force of habit. We fall into fixed patterns, saying the same phrases again and again without realizing it. Even in the most informal settings, we can often anticipate, almost word for word, what people will pray. This predictability results not from careful adherence to a prescribed form, but from unnoticed habits.

In the early days of automobiles, the narrow wheels of cars gradually wore deep trenches into the muddy roads. These ditches often went unnoticed until a driver wanted to turn left or right in an unusual location. The depth of the tracks made it difficult to steer out of the path that had been cut by so many other drivers.

As in many areas of life, Christians tend to fall into ruts in their religious practices. Unfortunately, these habits are difficult to break, especially in the area of prayer. Consider the familiar opening line, "Father, thank you for this day." We hear this sentence in prayer nearly everywhere we go. Yet, how often do any of us actually stop and give thanks from deep within our hearts when we hear these words?

Many of the main elements in our prayers fall into this category. When we do not think about what we are going to say, we simply repeat the same meaningless phrases again and again. Freedom in prayer can actually make us prisoners of habits that rob us of the wonder of talking with God. As a result, we must guard against an informality that leads us into an unrewarding formalism of its own.

A second difficulty with overemphasizing freedom comes to light

	PSALM 30	PSALM 32
INTRODUCTORY SUMMARY	1-3	1-2
CALL TO PRAISE	4-5	11
NARRATIVE ACCOUNT	6-12a	3-9
VIEWS OF FUTURE	12b	10

Fig. 10.2. Common Elements of Narrative Praise

when the prayers in the Bible are compared with the spontaneous prayers of many Christians. Although the Bible contains examples of spontaneity (e.g., Neh. 2:4-5), it is not the hallmark of most biblical prayers. The Psalms for instance, show a deep concern for structure and content. Most of the Psalms follow recurring patterns. For instance, Psalms 4 and 5 essentially follow the same outline (see fig. 10.1).

Both of these psalms begin with an invocation followed by a lament, petition, and statements of confidence. These two psalms are examples of a large group called "Psalms of Lament." In Old Testament times, the people of God used this basic form of prayer whenever they suffered. The model for such prayers was planned beforehand and adapted to the immediate circumstances.

A comparison of Psalms 30 and 32 reveals another type of structure (see fig. 10.2).

These psalms begin with an introductory summary followed by a call to praise, a narrative account, and a view toward the future. These two psalms are examples of another large group called "Narrative Praise." They too follow a preconceived pattern.

The Psalms also indicate that prayers may be planned down to the last letter. The words of the Psalms were often used in specific situations. For instance, when David had finished preparing for the temple, he prayed:

> Praise be to you, O LORD,
>   God of our father Israel,
>   from everlasting to everlasting.
> Yours, O LORD, is the greatness and the power
>   and the glory and the majesty and the splendor,
>   for everything in heaven and earth is yours.
> Yours, O LORD, is the kingdom;
>   you are exalted as head over all.

Wealth and honor come from you;
    you are the ruler of all things.
In your hands are strength and power
    to exalt and give strength to all.
Now, our God, we give you thanks,
    and praise your glorious name (1 Chron. 29:10-13).

This prayer is a combination of quotations from several different psalms. Similarly, when Solomon neared the end of his prayer at the dedication of the temple, he quoted a portion of Psalm 132:

Now arise, O LORD God, and come to your resting place,
    you and the ark of your might.
May your priests, O LORD God, be clothed with salvation,
    may your saints rejoice in your goodness.
O LORD God, do not reject your anointed one.
Remember the kindnesses promised to David
    your servant (2 Chron. 6:41-42).

In the New Testament, as well, Jesus quoted directly from Psalm 22:1 when He was on the cross:

My God, my God, why have you forsaken me? (Matt. 27:46b).

In these events, the words of the Psalms were used as guides for prayer. Those who prayed were genuine and sincere, no doubt, but the words had been known beforehand and simply adapted to the time of prayer.

Consequently, Christians must not overestimate the value of freedom in prayer. Not only does it hinder our ability to break with unconscious habits; it also puts us at odds with many biblical models for prayer. A desire for freedom can be positive, but it must be balanced by a proper appreciation of form.

Form in Prayer

Just as some Christians emphasize the value of freedom in prayer, others find that forethought makes their communication with God more fruitful. This outlook is usually based on the conviction that

God is worthy of careful preparation on the part of those who wish to speak with Him. As our Creator and Redeemer, God deserves to be treated with the highest respect. Every believer knows that God should not be taken lightly. His majesty is awe-inspiring:

> Praise the LORD, O my soul;
> all my inmost being, praise his holy name.
> Praise the LORD, O my soul,
> and forget not all his benefits.
>
> He forgives all my sins
> and heals all my diseases;
> he redeems my life from the pit
> and crowns me with love and compassion.
> He satisfies my desires with good things,
> so that my youth is renewed like the eagle's (Ps. 103:1-5).

Even the sinless creatures of heaven are overcome by the holiness of God:

> Holy, holy, holy is the LORD Almighty;
> the whole earth is full of his glory (Isa. 6:3).

While God is our friend, He is also our King. He is the Master who reigns above all others. For this reason, planning our prayers is quite appropriate.

I once testified before a governor's commission in the state of Virginia. The commission was discussing whether public welfare funds should finance abortions. The men and women on the commission exerted a great deal of influence on policies in the state, and I had a chance to speak to them. Needless to say, I did not simply stand up and say whatever came to mind; I prepared beforehand. I carefully organized my thoughts and chose my words with precision. I endeavored to express myself as clearly and persuasively as possible.

At one time or another we have all been in situations where we felt the need to plan what we would say. If we take such care when addressing human beings, how much more appropriate it is to think ahead when addressing our almighty God. To be sure, we need not think ahead in all our prayers, but we should plan our communication with God when our circumstances allow.

Forethought in prayer has many benefits. In the first place, following a preconceived outline can help us keep the elements of our prayers balanced. One purpose of the Lord's Prayer (Matt. 6:9-13) is to insure that all the legitimate elements of communication with God are balanced with each other. When we are tempted to spend all of our time focusing on our needs, we remember the opening lines of Jesus' prayer:

> Our Father in heaven,
> hallowed be your name,
> your kingdom come,
> your will be done
>   on earth as it is in heaven (vv. 9-10).

If we think that God does not care to know about our desires, we remember,

> Give us today our daily bread (v. 11).

When we fail to confess our sins, another portion of the model reminds us,

> Forgive us our debts,
>   as we also have forgiven our debtors (v. 12).

When we forget the future, we recall,

> And lead us not into temptation,
> but deliver us from the evil one (v. 13).

The Lord's Prayer demonstrates how a planned outline can produce well-balanced communication with God.

In the second place, planning the actual words of prayer can also be beneficial. The prayers of the Psalms have been highly treasured by the church because of their beauty and depth. The psalmists were skilled writers who used their abilities in service to God, and their prayers were kept for us that we might use them in our own lives. Consider the beauty of Psalm 50:1-2:

> The Mighty One, God, the LORD,
>   speaks and summons the earth

> from the rising of the sun to the place where it sets.
> From Zion, perfect in beauty,
>> God shines forth.

The words of another psalm also portray careful and creative use of language in prayer:

> How lovely is your dwelling place,
>> O LORD Almighty!
> My soul yearns, even faints,
>> for the courts of the LORD;
> my heart and my flesh cry out
>> for the living God.
>
> Even the sparrow has found a home,
>> and the swallow a nest for herself,
>> where she may have her young—
> a place near your altar,
>> O LORD Almighty, my King and my God (Ps. 84:1-3).

Using words of the Psalms and other prayers in the Bible can deeply enrich the beauty and value of our communication with God.

Beyond this, many other collections of prayers outside of Scripture can be useful. Though these are not divinely inspired, they can, nevertheless, help us express ourselves more adequately. I have a number of friends raised in informal churches who find that using prayer books and hymnals adds a wonderful dimension to their communication with God. The sense of awe and reverence created by the beautiful words and phrases found in these collections cannot be matched. When we use these resources, we are in effect being led in prayer by some of the greatest teachers and leaders of the church. Just as a well-composed song can inspire and lift our hearts, well-written prayers can move our souls to fuller communication with God.

Planned prayers are valuable in many ways, but they also present a number of dangers to be avoided. One common problem is the ease with which prewritten prayers can be read with insincerity. Many Christians know how easy it is to slip into a meaningless ritual when using formal prayers. How many times do little children mean what they say when they repeat, "God is great. God is good . . ."?

Even adults fall easily into the trap of simply repeating the Lord's Prayer on Sunday morning. These tendencies sound a stern warning to us. No matter how beautifully prepared the prayer may be, it is worthless unless the petitioners make the words their own. Prepared prayers must become the prayers of our hearts.

The other major danger involved with planned prayers is their inability to reflect the immediate needs we face. Several years ago, I had prepared an opening prayer for Sunday worship. I had written it to express the joy and wonder of worshiping God. Just before the service, however, I received word that a well-known church member had died of cancer the night before. In the light of this immediate concern, I had to discard my prayer. Instead, I prayed about the immediate sorrow and mourning the church was suffering. It would have been a serious mistake to continue with what I had planned when circumstances had changed so drastically. So it is whenever we pray. Prepared prayers are valuable, but they can easily be discordant with what we are going through at the time.

One reason for the many different prayers in the Psalms is the variety of circumstances they reflect. No one form or set of prepared words can deal with all the circumstances God's people face. Psalm 7, for instance, is concerned with a false accusation:

> O LORD my God, if I have done this
>   and there is guilt on my hands—
> if I have done evil to him who is at peace with me
>   or without cause have robbed my foe—
> then let my enemy pursue and overtake me (vv. 3-5a).

Psalm 83 is concerned with the attacks of enemies:

> "Come," they say, "let us destroy them as a nation,
>   that the name of Israel be remembered no more" (v. 4).

Psalm 34 is a praise to God for a personal matter:

> I sought the LORD, and he answered me;
>   he delivered me from all my fears (v. 4).

Whereas Psalm 124 is a celebration of national importance:

> If the LORD had not been on our side—
>   let Israel say—
> If the LORD had not been on our side
>   when men attacked us,
> when their anger flared against us,
>   they would have swallowed us alive (vv. 1-3).

Believers of old were not satisfied simply to repeat the words of others when these words did not match their own situations. They knew the importance of offering prayers related to the circumstances at hand.

Form, like freedom, has advantages and disadvantages. By using prepared prayers, we may achieve a balance and expression in our communication with God that will please Him greatly. Yet, we may also fall victim to insincerity and irrelevance if we are not vigilant to pray from our hearts and in the light of our current circumstances.

If form and freedom both have advantages and disadvantages, how are we to improve our communication in prayer? In a word, the answer is *variety*. Most Christians, depending on their background and present experiences, tend to think that one kind of prayer is better than the other. Unfortunately, these personal preferences can get out of hand. I have heard Christians laugh at a fellow believer's prayer because it did not measure up to the refinement of their written prayers. I have heard others mock their neighbors for reading their prayers from a book. We should avoid both of these attitudes.

One of the best ways to keep our prayers vibrant and meaningful is to vary between spontaneity and formality. We need to be able to use written prayers and to write our own prayers at times. Yet, we also need to know the freedom of spontaneous encounter with God, never forgetting that He hears us because of His grace at work in our hearts, not because of our eloquent words. As we develop the ability to approach prayer in both ways, we will find our communication with God growing in depth and wonder (see fig. 10.3).

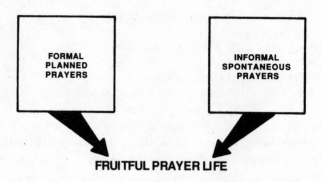

Fig. 10.3. Variety in Prayer

Discussion Questions

1. Of what value are freedom and spontaneity in prayer? What dangers are present in these kinds of prayers? How can these dangers be avoided?

2. Of what value are form and forethought in prayer? What dangers are present in these kinds of prayers? How can these dangers be avoided?

3. Why is it helpful to vary our prayers between form and freedom?

Exercises

1. Make a list of three situations in which you would feel free to speak spontaneously. Then list three situations in which you would think it necessary to plan what you would say. What are the differences? How is prayer similar to these different situations?

2. Discuss the holiness of God spontaneously and develop an informal description of His holiness. Then read the hymn "Holy, Holy, Holy." Compare and contrast your informal discussion with the hymn. Which is better? Why?

3. Write a four-or-five-sentence prayer in which you use the words of biblical psalms or hymns. As much as possible, use the form below.

O God, You are _____
(description of God from a hymn or psalm)

_____.

We lift our voices in praise. _____
(Insert a section of praise from Ps. 92, 100, or 150.)

_____.

We praise You for _____
(Insert another section from Ps. 92, 100, or 150.)

_____.

How we worship You, for You are _____

_____
(description of God from a hymn or psalm)

_____.

Extended Exercise

Three times this week choose a psalm or a hymn and read it in a prayer. You may find the form in exercise 3 helpful.

11

Communicating Petitions

When I was a teen-ager, one of my favorite forms of entertainment was listening to the radio. I particularly enjoyed a program called "Request Line." Every Tuesday and Thursday night, I would tune in to the local radio station and listen as the announcer invited callers to request their favorite songs and to dedicate them to their friends. A call lasted only about fifteen seconds, but the program was great fun, especially when a friend dedicated a song to someone you knew.

Request line programs are fine entertainment, but they make poor models for prayer. Sadly, we Christians often pray as if we have just dialed God on a request line. We simply reel off to God all the things we want, as quickly as they come to mind.

A young pastor once asked for prayer requests during a Sunday morning worship service. He hoped that a few members would share their needs so that he could remember them in the pastoral prayer. Much to his surprise, however, the members of the congregation made one request after another. Again and again they told of needs and problems. "This is wonderful," the pastor thought. Then he looked down at his watch and realized he had only two minutes left to pray for all of these requests. In a panic, he simply read quickly through his list: "Lord, take care of . . . and bless . . . and take care of . . . and bless. . . ."

Many of us frequently offer petitions in this manner. In prayer groups, we spend so much time sharing requests with each other that we must hurry through the actual prayer. Even privately, our prayer lists grow so long that we are unable to give much time to each request. We are tempted simply to crumple the list in our hands and say, "Lord, you know all our needs. Please just take care of them." In the back of our minds we know that prayer must be more than quickly reviewing a long list of names and items. Are there better ways of communicating our needs to God? What can we do differently?

Persuasive Urgency

First, we must realize that nothing is wrong with making numerous, brief requests in prayer. The Lord's Prayer, for instance, contains five requests in just five verses (Matt. 6:9-13). Solomon's prayer at the dedication of the temple has an even longer series of petitions (1 Kings 8:22-53). To ask for many things in prayer is quite acceptable. Nevertheless, if this approach dominates our prayers over a long period of time, it can lead to the neglect of some important dimensions of effective communication with God. The Bible gives helpful alternatives to the prayer request line.

Jesus' teaching on prayer makes it clear that prayer may be much more urgent and persuasive than rapid-fire requests. He once told a parable to illustrate how urgency should be a vital dimension of our prayers:

> Then he said to them, "Suppose one of you has a friend, and he goes to him at midnight and says, 'Friend, lend me three loaves of bread, because a friend of mine on a journey has come to me, and I have nothing to set before him.'
>
> "Then the one inside answers, 'Don't bother me. The door is already locked, and my children are with me in bed. I can't get up and give you anything.' I tell you, though he will not get up and give him the bread because he is his friend, yet because of

the man's persistence he will get up and give him as much as he needs" (Luke 11:5-8).

Jesus describes a man who had unexpected overnight guests. He went to his neighbor in the middle of the night to ask for some bread. The neighbor's family was in bed and he refused to get up. In response, the man made his request with such urgent persistence that the neighbor finally got up and gave him the bread. Then Jesus concludes:

> So I say to you: Ask and it will be given to you; seek and you will find; knock and the door will be opened to you. For everyone who asks receives; he who seeks finds; and to him who knocks, the door will be opened (Luke 11:9-10).

As Jesus' concluding remark demonstrates, God is intensely concerned with the needs of His children (Matt. 6:25-33). Yet, the parable also teaches that we have a responsibility to be urgent and persistent in our prayers.

Many prayers in the Psalms confirm this point of view. When the psalmists faced difficulties, they took care to express their intense feelings in prayer. In Psalm 69, we find the prayer of one who has been judged falsely. He says of himself,

> I am forced to restore
> what I did not steal (v. 4b).

In the midst of this troubling situation, he continues to trust God. He is sure of God's love and His perfect timing:

> But I pray to you, O LORD,
> in time of your favor;
> in your great love, O God,
> answer me with your sure salvation (v. 13).

Yet, even with this confidence, the psalmist expresses urgency in His petition. He does not simply pray, "Lord, please take care of my problem." Instead, he communicates his deep longings in the situation. Notice how dramatically and urgently he makes his petition known:

Rescue me from the mire,
   do not let me sink;
deliver me from those who hate me,
   from the deep waters (v. 14).

Similarly, in Psalm 144:2 we find an expression of confidence in the love of God:

He is my loving God and my fortress,
   my stronghold and my deliverer,
my shield, in whom I take refuge,
   who subdues peoples under me.

Even so, intense requests accompany this confidence:

Reach down your hand from on high;
   deliver me and rescue me
from the mighty waters,
   from the hands of foreigners (Ps. 144:7).

Urgent pleas fill the pages of the Psalms. The psalmists do not tell God what they need as succinctly as possible. They elaborate dramatically on their requests, demonstrating their intense feelings.

Jesus Himself is a model of urgency in prayer. In the Garden of Gethsemane, He repeatedly turned to His heavenly Father with His earnest request. Luke describes how intensely Jesus petitioned the Father:

He prayed more earnestly, and his sweat was like drops of blood falling to the ground (Luke 22:44).

Jesus not only taught us to be urgent in prayer; He also modeled what it means to pray in this manner.

In ordinary conversations, we are accustomed to expressing our desires in ways that are intense and persuasive. One evening I received a call from some friends whom I had not seen for two years. They wanted me to come for a visit. I was eager to see them. But the trip involved a cross-country flight and would take several days out of my busy schedule. Initially I declined the invitation. But they insisted, "You simply must come. We have something very impor-

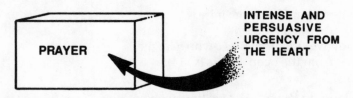

Fig. 11.1. Urgency in Prayer

tant to talk over with you." After several hours of conversation, I began to realize how urgently they wanted to see me. In response to their intense desire, I finally boarded a plane and went to visit them. In our relationships with people, we know how to relate our urgent desires to others quite effectively.

Unfortunately, however, the same cannot be said of our prayers. Regularly, we face situations that desperately need God's intervention—family problems, sickness, hunger—to name only a few. Yet, how do we usually handle these circumstances? Too often we pray as if they were trivial to us. We treat international conflict on a par with getting good grades in school. We spend more time in prayer about an insignificant job promotion than we do about a neighbor's serious illness. As a result, our petitions often lack all signs of urgency. Though at times a simple sentence or phrase will suffice, we must be careful not to formulate all our petitions in this manner. Following the examples of Christ and the psalmists, we must learn how to communicate our urgency to God in prayer (see fig. 11.1).

Building a Case

In ordinary conversations, we often express urgency by setting forth reasons why our requests should be met. We may even seek the advice of others and plan beforehand what we want to say.

The story is told of two boys who had mastered communication on this level. They wanted to hike up a mountain path not far from home, but they suspected that their parents would not permit them to go. So they spent an entire morning together creating a list of reasons why they should be allowed to climb that mountain. Later in the day, they read their twenty-five arguments to their parents.

When the parents heard the boys respectfully but fervently presenting one argument after another, their hearts melted and they permitted the boys to go. The boys wanted to take that hike, and they
figured out how to do it; they supported their request with carefully
constructed reasons.

In similar ways God has invited us to build a case before Him in
prayer. Instead of simply asking for things as quickly as possible,
biblical figures frequently took the time to create an elaborate ration-
ale for their requests. Consider the example of Abraham. When he
learned that God intended to destroy the cities of Sodom and
Gomorrah, he did not merely ask, "Lord, please do not destroy the
cities." Instead, he accompanied his request with persuasive
reasoning:

> Will you really sweep it away and not spare the place for the
> sake of the fifty righteous people in it? Far be it from you to do
> such a thing—to kill the righteous with the wicked, treating the
> righteous and the wicked alike. Far be it from you! Will not the
> Judge of all the earth do right? (Gen. 18:24b-25).

Abraham called attention to the fact that God, as the Judge of all the
earth, would not destroy the righteous along with the wicked of the
cities. The patriarch built a strong case for his request, and the Lord
heard him. He offered his petition with humility, but also with a
determination to support his desire as well as he could. His prayer
stands as an example for all of us.

We can also find this sort of reasoning in many psalms. Psalm 69,
for instance, presents requests but also gives supporting reasons. In
verses 16-18 we find three closely related petitions, each of which is
accompanied by a supportive remark:

> Answer me, O LORD, out of the goodness of your love;
>   in your great mercy turn to me.
> Do not hide your face from your servant;
>   answer me quickly, for I am in trouble.
> Come near and rescue me;
>   redeem me because of my foes.

In the first place, the psalmist asked God to answer "out of the
goodness of your love." God's loving character was a support for

the petition. He asked God to answer quickly because "I am in trouble." The psalmist's own condition was another solid reason for his request. He also cried for rescue "because of my foes." The enemies around him were a good reason for God to answer. This kind of support for petitions appears repeatedly throughout the Psalms. In fact, it is unusual to find a psalmist asking for something without also offering at least one reason why it should be granted.

Even the extensive laments found in many psalms are, in effect, a way of building a case before God. In Psalm 22:6-8 we read:

> But I am a worm and not a man,
>   scorned by men and despised by the people.
> All who see me mock me;
>   they hurl insults, shaking their heads:
> "He trusts in the LORD;
>   let the LORD rescue him.
> Let him deliver him,
>   since he delights in him."

These words do not simply express a troubled spirit; they also offer a reason why God should come to the aid of the psalmist. In effect, he is saying, "Will You continue to allow wicked people to mock Your child and Your Word?" Whenever the psalmists raise a lament, they are demonstrating their urgency by building a convincing case for their petitions.

I should add a word of caution at this point. We must be careful not to turn this legitimate dimension of prayer into an occasion for arrogance before God. When we build a case in prayer, we are not informing God of anything He does not already know. Nor are we twisting His arm to do something He does not care to do. On the contrary, when we turn to God in prayer, it must be as creatures speaking to the almighty Creator of the universe. Giving reasons for our requests does not call into question His wisdom or sovereignty; it simply demonstrates a high regard for Him.

Moreover, once God has acted, we must humbly accept His holy and wise decision. When the first child of Bathsheba was on the verge of death, David prayed diligently for him. Yet, once the child was dead, David explained to his servants:

While the child was still alive, I fasted and wept. I thought,

"Who knows? The LORD may be gracious to me and let the child live." But now that he is dead, why should I fast? Can I bring him back again? I will go to him, but he will not return to me (2 Sam. 12:22-23).

Even in the wake of a grievous loss, David humbly bowed before God's sovereign will. Similarly, when Paul prayed for relief from a problem, he continued until God's will for him was plain:

Three times I pleaded with the Lord to take it away from me. But he said to me, "My grace is sufficient for you, for my power is made perfect in weakness." Therefore I will boast all the more gladly about my weaknesses, so that Christ's power may rest on me (2 Cor. 12:8-9).

Like David and Paul, we too should recognize that building a case before God must be balanced with respect for God as our sovereign Lord.

Even so, we can hardly overestimate the value of learning how to support petitions in prayer. It can transform our prayers in many ways. Two benefits are particularly significant. First, it provides a way of communicating with God when we have little idea of what to say. One evening I received a message by phone that the daughter of some good friends had been diagnosed as having spinal meningitis. The doctors gave her only a short while to live. The church immediately began to organize prayer meetings all over the city. When my group assembled that evening, everyone was terribly upset. We looked at each other and wondered what to do. God already knew that we wanted her to be well. How could we pray when all we could say was, "Please, please, please . . . "? What words could possibly convey our feelings? Then someone suggested that we offer to God all the reasons we could muster for Him to show mercy to the child. The idea was well received, and the whole group began mounting one reason upon another. By the end of the hour, we all felt some sense of relief in knowing that we had communicated with God as effectively as we could. We had done our best to offer persuasive prayers—the only action we could take for the sick child. Happily, a few weeks later God miraculously brought the little girl to health, and today she lives a perfectly normal life. That

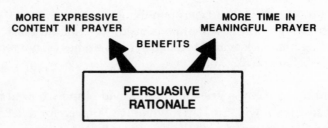

Fig. 11.2. The Value of Building a Case

event convinced me of the importance of building a case before God. It allows us to express ourselves when simple requests seem so inadequate.

Building a case also gives us an ability to spend longer periods of time in fruitful prayer. Many Christians wish they could spend more time praying but find that their minds wander and their hearts grow weary after only a few minutes. After all, how long can you keep on lifting up one request after another without succumbing to meaningless repetition? Many factors explain the ability of some Christians to pray more than others. Undoubtedly, some believers are simply more adept at praying, just as some are more adept at singing or teaching. Nevertheless, learning how to build a case can contribute significantly to every believer's ability to spend longer periods of time in effective prayer.

When I pastored a church, the church leaders customarily met for a time of extended prayer on Friday night and Saturday morning about once every three months. We usually spent that time focusing our attention on one or two needs in the church. For one, two, even three hours at a time, we concentrated on a few specific items of prayer. As I think back, those days are still among my most memorable prayer experiences. How were we able to pray for so long without resorting to innumerable lists of concerns? How could we pray for hours about one request without falling into mindless repetition? The answer is simple. We spent time developing and presenting extensive support for our petitions. One after another, the leaders of the church built their cases before God. We never became bored or weary in those prayers. We communicated effectively with God for hours by explaining and supporting our requests.

So it is that Christians may demonstrate urgency in prayer. As we make requests of God, we should frequently fill our prayers with extensive reasoning and support in favor of the petitions. When this is our regular practice, our communication with God will benefit in countless ways (see fig.11.2).

Kinds of Support

What specific kinds of support can we legitimately offer to God? From what persuasive resources may we draw? How may we order these thoughts in ways that please God? In many respects answers to these questions will vary individually and one particular scheme will not suffice for all situations. Still, we can make some general observations that yield several helpful ideas.

We can divide the kinds of support we may offer into three categories. First, we may back up some requests by reflection on God's people. Second, we may base requests on considerations of the world around us. Third, we may support petitions by an appeal to the character and Word of God. These three foci—God's people, the world, and God and His Word—are fundamental elements in providing support for petitions.

We find an exemplary prayer containing all three of these elements in Exodus 32. After seeing the golden calf, God determined to destroy the people of Israel, but Moses offered an urgent and persuasive prayer. The persuasive elements of Moses' prayer focus on three concerns. First, Moses reflects on the people of God:

> "O LORD," he said, "why should your anger burn against your people, whom you brought out of Egypt with great power and a mighty hand?" (Exod. 32:11b).

Crucial to his question is the phrase "your people." Moses knew that the Israelites were not ordinary people in the eyes of God. They were the apple of His eye and dear to His heart. For this reason, Moses built a case for God to forgive by focusing on the special character of the people of God.

This theme appears throughout the Bible. In Psalm 90:12 we read,

> Teach us to number our days aright,
>   that we may gain a heart of wisdom.

Why does the psalmist request the ability to assess the brevity of life?—in order that he and his associates may gain wisdom. A plea for acceptance and forgiveness in Psalm 69:17 is also supported by an appeal on behalf of God's people:

> Do not hide your face from your servant;
>   answer me quickly, for I am in trouble.

The psalmist points to his own troubled condition as a support for his request. A focus on ourselves and others as the people of God can be an effective way of building a case in prayer.

The second way in which Moses supported His request in Exodus 32 was by drawing attention to the world around him:

> Why should the Egyptians say, "It was with evil intent that he brought them out, to kill them in the mountains and to wipe them off the face of the earth"? Turn from your fierce anger; relent and do not bring disaster on your people (Exod. 32:12).

Moses' point of view is clear. God's destruction of His people would produce an unacceptable result in the world. The Egyptians would mock and scoff at the Lord and His people. Moses knew that God did not deliver Israel just to give the Egyptians opportunity to laugh at what He had done. On the contrary, God had performed His signs and wonders to bring glory to Himself. So, Moses appealed on the basis of the bad effects that the destruction of Israel would cause in the world around him.

The Psalms often mention events in the world as support for petitions. In Psalm 55 the psalmist prays,

> Confuse the wicked, O Lord,
>   confound their speech (Ps. 55:9a).

Yet, why should God confuse the wicked?

> . . . for I see violence and strife in the city.
> Day and night they prowl about on its walls;
>   malice and abuse are within it (Ps. 55:9b-10).

The psalmist gives the conditions of the world surrounding him as a basis for his request. Similarly, in Psalm 74:18 we read,

> Remember how the enemy has mocked you, O LORD,
>   how foolish people have reviled your name.

The psalmist pleads with God to hear him because of what his foes are doing. Once again he derives support for a petition from external conditions. A focus on the external world in prayer can take many forms. Whatever the case, a concern with the world around us can also be a significant way of building a case before God.

Third, Moses turned to God and His Word as a basis for his request:

> Remember your servants Abraham, Isaac and Israel, to whom you swore by your own self: "I will make your decendants as numerous as the stars in the sky and I will give your descendants all this land I promised them, and it will be their inheritance forever" (Exod. 32:13).

Moses recalled the promises of God to the patriarchs in an effort to build support for his plea. He knew that God would be true to His ancient promises. So Moses cited the Word of God as a final appeal.

We can also find this kind of support in the Psalms. Many times the psalmists ask God to deal with them according to His covenant faithfulness and mercy. In no uncertain terms, Psalm 74 implores:

> Do not hand over the life of your dove to wild beasts;
>   do not forget the lives of your afflicted people forever.
> Have regard for your covenant (vv. 19-20a).

In Psalm 119:149, we read,

> Hear my voice in accordance with your love;
>   preserve my life, O LORD, according to your laws.

Again, in a more daring fashion, the psalmist says,

> O Lord, where is your former great love,
>   which in your faithfulness you swore to David? (Ps. 89:49).

As children of God, we may appeal to God's character and His Word

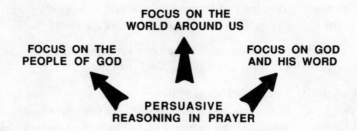

Fig. 11.3. Dimensions of Prayerful Support

as we pray. God is faithful to His nature and His promises. By appealing to God and His Word, we may build a strong case in support of our petitions (see fig. 11.3).

In this chapter we have seen that we are to offer urgent and persuasive petitions to God. We may make our prayers compelling by building our cases in three main ways: (1) focusing on God's people, (2) focusing on the external world around us, and (3) focusing on God and His Word. When Moses availed himself of these resources, he received a wonderful response from God:

> Then the LORD relented and did not bring on his people the disaster he had threatened (Exod. 32:14).

As we increasingly make use of these divinely ordained means, we too will find our communication with God growing in effectiveness.

Discussion Questions

1. How do two examples of biblical prayers exhibit persuasive urgency? Describe the ways in which modern prayers often fail to resemble these models.

2. What does it mean to build a case in prayer? Cite some biblical examples of this. What dangers should we avoid in this area?

3. What are three major sources of support upon which we may draw in prayer?

Exercises

1. Choose a petition that is commonly offered in prayer and list five reasons why you think the request should be granted. Evaluate your reasons, building on God and His Word, the world around you, and the people of God.

2. Write a six-to-eight-sentence prayer in which you ask for one thing and support your requests with at least three reasons. As much as possible, use the form below as a guide.

O _____ ,
                              (divine name or title)

we come to You asking _____
                                                (Present petition.)

_____

_____

_____ .

We make this request because of Your people. We are _____

_____
            (Give support by an appeal on behalf of God's people.)

_____ .

We call upon You because of the world around us. The world

_____
               (Give support from circumstances in the world.)

_____

_____

_____ .

We also make this request because of Your character. You are

_____
              (Give support from God's character or His Word.)

_____

_____

_____ .

Hear our prayer, O Lord. We honor You, _____
                                          (divine name or title)

_____,

for Your generous hand. Amen.

Extended Exercise

During the next week spend two or three times in prayer asking for
only one thing. Be sure to support that request with persuasive
reasoning. You may find it helpful to use the form suggested above
in exercise 2.

12
Communicating Gratitude

Now thank we all our God
With heart and hands and voices,
Who wondrous things hath done,
In whom his world rejoices;
Who from our mothers' arms,
Hath blessed us on our way
With countless gifts of love,
And still is ours today.
                    Martin Rinkart
                    1586-1649

Little children have an amazing ability to make adults laugh. Their insatiable curiosity, their irreverent questions, their unexpected poses, all have great power to delight. But despite the joy children bring, even the proudest parent has to admit that the halo slips at least now and then. We have all seen it. Aunt Sally offers little Joey a piece of candy. Joey snatches it from her hand. Mother calls from across the room, "Say thank you, honey." No response. "Say thank you, Joey!" She stands in front of him, frowning. "Say thank you right now or go to your room." Joey looks at the finger pointing toward the bedroom. He hesitates and drops his eyes to the ground. Then through his clenched teeth he forces a barely audible "Thanks," and runs out of the room. Showing gratitude does not come naturally to children. They have to learn how to do it, and parents spend a lot of time teaching them.

As strange as it may sound, showing gratitude does not come naturally to adults either. Most adults have learned how to be polite enough to thank their colleagues and friends for favors, but we tend to feel uncomfortable when we have to express sincere, deep-seated gratitude. If we have difficulty expressing gratitude to people we

151

can see and touch, how much more difficult it is to express thank-
fulness to our immortal, invisible God. Most Christians know that
God deserves our gratitude. We recognize, at least intellectually,
that He has given us everything we value, but often heartfelt
thanksgiving does not come easily. Effectively communicating our
gratitude to God is an art worthy to be learned. In this chapter we
will explore ways of expressing gratitude to God. Are there words to
convey effectively our thanksgiving? How can we communicate our
gratitude to God?

The Cause and Purpose of Gratitude

We say "Thank you" to each other for many different reasons.
Sometimes, we do it simply out of habit. The story is told of a young
woman who found herself saying "Thank you" a hundred times a
day, even when she did not mean it. Every time someone helped her
in the least, she thanked that person profusely. One day a police
officer scolded her severely for going over the speed limit. As he
handed her a speeding ticket, she responded with a big smile and a
hearty, "Thank you." Finally, one day a fellow office worker could
take it no longer. "Would you please stop saying 'Thank you' all the
time? I think I'll scream if you say it one more time." The young
woman sighed heavily, "I guess I do go a bit overboard. I'll do my
best to keep myself under control. Thank you." At that point a
deafening scream cut through the office!

Unfortunately, believers often express gratitude in prayer in the
same unconscious way. We go to God with thanks because we have
a habit of doing so. In fact, we are so accustomed to including a word
of thanksgiving in prayer that we tend to rely heavily on a few
standard phrases. "Thank you for the many things you have given
us. . . ." "Thank you for this day. . . ." "Thank you for sending
Your Son to save us from our sins. . . ."—to mention just a few.
None of these expressions is inappropriate. We should give thanks
for these wonderful gifts from God. But when these words simply
come to our lips automatically, they fail to reflect the true attitudes of
our hearts.

Scripture teaches that thanksgiving in prayer is to be a deep appreciation for what God has done for us. Often Christians become so entangled in the affairs of this life that the reality of God's blessing fades from their minds. At one time or another, most parents have experienced this kind of neglect from their children. They work hard, save, and sacrifice to buy them clothes and toys that sit in the closet because they do not quite match current trends. In a similar way, believers often overlook the gifts of God. We are constantly tempted to forget that God grants our every need. So we must put forth a concerted effort to appreciate His blessings. This is why Paul said,

> Give thanks in all circumstances, for this is God's will for you in Christ Jesus (1 Thess. 5:18).

God is not far removed from our lives. When good comes our way, we must not explain it in terms of natural causes. We must appreciate it as the gift of the Creator Himself.

By understanding what it means to be thankful, we also begin to see the purpose of gratitude in prayer. The opening words of Psalm 30 offer a clear declaration of the purpose behind thanksgiving:

> I will exalt you, O LORD,
>   for you lifted me out of the depths
>   and did not let my enemies gloat over me (v. 1).

The psalmist has received a blessing from God, and his heart is filled with gratitude. Consequently, he devotes himself to exalting God through prayer. He seeks to make God's goodness evident through his words. We hear this same desire to magnify God reverberating through Psalm 34:1-2:

> I will extol the LORD at all times;
>   his praise will always be on my lips.
> My soul will boast in the LORD;
>   let the afflicted hear and rejoice.

In this passage the psalmist tells us his thanksgiving is designed to glorify the Lord. He even calls on others to join with him. The same motivation lies behind the opening of the Lord's Prayer:

> Hallowed be your name (Matt. 6:9c).

These passages teach that a central purpose for expressing gratitude is the exaltation of God through our words. In prayer we display the special and honorable place God occupies in our hearts because of what He has done.

When I served as director of church education, I gave an annual teachers' appreciation dinner. Throughout the year I would say a word of thanks to each teacher from time to time, but through this banquet I showed my gratitude in a special way. I arrived at the church early in the morning and spent most of the day preparing the meal, forbidding the teachers to help in any way. That evening I served the food I had prepared for them and their spouses. I didn't go to all that trouble because I enjoyed cooking so much. I gave the teachers the royal treatment in order to exalt them. I so appreciated their cooperative spirits and hard work that I wanted to demonstrate how special I thought they were. For the most part, I think they got the message.

In many ways this is what we do when we express gratitude in prayer. Thanksgiving shows appreciation for God. It is not an opportunity for a recital of a few cliches. It is not fulfilling an obligation because we fear we may appear ungrateful. Thanksgiving is a service intensely directed toward a person. We express gratitude in order to treat God with the respect and honor He deserves for the things He has done for us. From the ordinary to the spectacular, God is always concerned with our needs. So we put together, as it were, a banquet of words for Him. He is our guest, and we serve Him with tokens of our appreciation and admiration (see fig. 12.1).

Words of Gratitude

One of the problems many Christians face when they pray is a lack of words to express their appreciation for God. From the examples of others around us, we usually conceive of thanksgiving simply as saying, "Thank you" for this or that, depending on what specific blessing we have in mind. This kind of prayer is wholesome and acceptable when offered sincerely, but it does not begin to incorporate the many ways we may effectively express our gratitude

Fig. 12.1. The Purpose of Gratitude

to God. How long can we simply say "Thank you" without falling into boredom or insincerity? What alternative expressions can help us communicate the appreciation we have in our hearts? Answers to these questions abound, but one crucial means for expressing gratitude appears time and time again in the Psalms.

The psalmists primarily showed their appreciation for God by giving detailed accounts of what God had done for them. In fact, thanksgivings in the Psalms often take the form of stories. In Psalm 30:6-10, we find the psalmist giving an interesting account of recent events in his life:

> When I felt secure, I said,
>   "I will never be shaken."
> O LORD, when you favored me,
>   you made my mountain stand firm;
> but when you hid your face,
>   I was dismayed.
>
> To you, O LORD, I called;
>   to the Lord I cried for mercy:
> "What gain is there in my destruction,
>   if I go down into the pit?
> Will the dust praise you?
>   Will it proclaim your faithfulness?
> Hear, O LORD, and be merciful to me;
>   O LORD, be my help."

Notice the detail with which the psalmist speaks of his experience. He describes how he had taken the blessings of God as an opportunity to fall into pride. As a result, God withdrew His protection and all sorts of trouble ensued. In the midst of this trouble, the psalmist called out with persuasive petitions, and the Lord heard him. Reflecting on these events, the psalmist does not merely say a quick "Thank You for Your help, Lord." He expresses thanks in this psalm by taking time to detail God's mercy toward him.

Psalm 34 adopts a similar pattern. The psalmist describes a blessing from God several times to those around him:

> I sought the LORD, and he answered me;
>> he delivered me from all my fears.
> Those who look to him are radiant;
>> their faces are never covered with shame.
> This poor man called, and the LORD heard him;
>> he saved him out of all his troubles.
> The angel of the LORD encamps around those who fear him,
>> and he delivers them (vv. 4-7).

In Psalm 18, we find another story of thanks, but this one has an important variation. The psalmist speaks of the trouble he faced in his own life and how God answered his prayer:

> In my distress I called to the LORD;
>> I cried to my God for help.
> From his temple he heard my voice;
>> my cry came before him, into his ears (v. 6).

Beyond this, however, he relates his own experience to a well-known story from Scripture. His deliverance paralleled the deliverance of Israel at the Red Sea:

> The earth trembled and quaked,
>> and the foundations of the mountains shook;
>> they trembled because he was angry.
> Smoke rose from his nostrils;
>> consuming fire came from his mouth,
>> burning coals blazed out of it.
> He parted the heavens and came down;
>> dark clouds were under his feet (vv. 7-9).

By relating his own life to the event of the Red Sea, the psalmist sheds light on the magnificence of what God had done for him. As God acted in the past, so He acted in the psalmist's life. In this psalm no fewer than forty-two verses (Ps. 18:4-45) are devoted to telling and retelling the story of God's actions.

When I was a pastor, I would visit members of my church when they entered the hospital and again when they returned home. Once they were home, I would ask the former patients to lead in prayer at the end of our visit. Usually, they would give a quick word of thanks and then move on to a list of needs—help with the bills, patience with the children, an increase of strength. However, I remember one exceptional visit. The mother of a church member had come home after undergoing treatment for cancer. As usual, I went to vist her and asked her to pray. Much to my surprise, she did not pray as others had. Instead, she told a story. She talked about God's care for her through the discovery of the affliction, His comfort in her times of fear, and His sustaining hand through the pain she had suffered. She went on to describe the kind spirit of her doctors, the opportunities she had been given to share her faith, the joy of coming home, and the thrill of hoping that she had conquered her disease. She also reflected for a moment on a few stories of Jesus' healing ministry that had become dear to her. After telling God about these events, she simply stopped and said, "Amen."

I was dumbfounded. She had prayed without asking for a single thing. Her prayer had consisted solely of a story of what God had done in her life. That day drastically changed my approach to prayer. Through this woman's example, I began to discover the joy of expressing gratitude to God by telling Him stories from my own life and describing how they remind me of His mighty acts in the Bible.

Every believer has a story to tell God, for He always performs wonders for His children—recovery from an illness, the resolution of a family problem, the deliverance of a friend from some kind of trouble. God invites us to come to Him and tell Him our story. To be sure, He already knows the blessings He has given us. We do not inform Him of anything new. Instead, we tell our story to give Him the pleasure of enjoying our gratitude. As a loving Father, God takes great delight in hearing stories of thanksgiving from His children.

Fig. 12.2. Stories of Gratitude

Recently, we gave a birthday party for our daughter at the local skating rink. She had a number of friends at the party and obviously had a good time. At bedtime I sat next to her and asked if she had enjoyed the party. "Sure," she responded. But I wanted to hear more. So I said, "Tell me what you liked about it." "I liked everything," she said quickly. Still not satisfied, I inquired further, "Can't you tell me a little more?" I wanted to know that she appreciated the effort her mother and I had made. Soon she got the idea and began to tell me about the afternoon. I sat and listened as she told me one episode after another. She may not have realized it, but all that time my daughter was saying, "Thank you," to me. I felt good knowing that the party had meant a lot to her.

In much the same way, Christians often think that a quick word or two sufficiently expresses gratitude for God's good gifts. Yet, from the examples of the Psalms, we see that God desires more from us. We can communicate our gratitude more fully by telling stories of His marvelous work in our lives. When we take the time to tell God the story of what He has done, we exalt Him and give Him the kind of thanksgiving He deserves (see fig. 12.2).

The Results of Gratitude

Having considered the purpose of gratitude and one way to express it, we may still wonder what results when believers express their gratitude to God. Will giving thanks to God in these ways have any effect on our lives? The outcome of saying "Thank you" to God not only is a pleasure and delight for God. It benefits us as well.

Taking the time to demonstrate our gratitude in prayer can be a source of encouragement when the burdens of life weigh heavily on us. It is difficult not to be overwhelmed at times by the evil that constantly confronts us. We see oppression and war on the international scene. We hear of violence and trouble in our cities. We fall prey to schemes of others in the marketplace. We encounter neighbors who are rude and inconsiderate. Even in the church, the actions of fellow Christians trouble us. Beyond this, we also look at ourselves and are sorely disappointed. Our lack of power to overcome personal problems frustrates us. Our own propensity toward selfishness perplexes us. We look at how little we have accomplished with our lives and wonder where all the time has gone. With these thoughts constantly bombarding us, it is no wonder that Christians are often weighed down under disappointment and discouragement. Happily, however, expressing gratitude in prayer can often be an effective way of overcoming these feelings.

In the Psalms a consistent portrait emerges as a result of thanksgiving. Invariably, the psalmists are deeply strengthened and encouraged. After the story of deliverance in Psalm 30 we read:

> You turned my wailing into dancing;
>> you removed my sackcloth and clothed me with joy,
> that my heart may sing to you and not be silent.
> O LORD my God, I will give you thanks
>> forever (vv. 11-12).

The psalmist rejoices that God has reversed his situation. Notice how tremendous his joy is. He is not merely relieved or quietly comforted in his soul. Joy so overflows from his heart that he cannot sit still. He dances before the Lord.

Another expression of thanksgiving in the Psalms has a slightly different result. After recounting the blessing of God, the psalmist turns to those around him and says:

> Taste and see that the LORD is good;
>> blessed is the man who takes refuge in him.

Fear the LORD, you his saints,
    for those who fear him lack nothing.
The lions may grow weak and hungry,
    but those who seek the LORD lack no good
        thing (Ps. 34:8-10).

In the original Old Testament context these words actually referred
to a feast the psalmist had prepared for his friends. It was the
practice of believers in those days to celebrate God's special blessings around a meal. As they ate the good food that had been
prepared for them, these believers had an opportunity to "Taste and
see that the LORD is good" (v. 8). As they savored the food they
could contemplate anew how God had been good to His people.
What they always knew to be a theoretical truth, they could know in
an immediate experiential way. God had shown His goodness.

A few years ago, I gave a series of lectures at a church conference
in Mexico. It was a grand experience in many ways, but I came down
with an illness which the Mexicans call *la enfermedad del turista* —
"tourist's sickness." In order to fulfill my teaching responsibilities, I
had to severely cut back on eating for the better part of three days.
Needless to say, by the end of the trip I was quite fatigued. My
attitude toward life was negative; it was difficult to see anything in a
positive light. On the way to the airport, I spent the night in the
home of some friends. The mother of the family could see that I was
very weak, so she insisted that I eat something. At first I was
reluctant, but at her urging I ate. With the first bite of that cheese
tortilla my hands began to tingle. Adrenalin started flowing, and my
whole body suddenly came back to life. Along with my body, my
spirits rose and my whole disposition brightened. Discouragement
and fatigue vanished, and I gained a new, positive outlook on life.

The same revitalization occurs when we take time to tell God
stories of gratitude. Though we may be worn down by the troubles
we face in this world, when we recount stories of God's mercy in our
lives and savor the wonder of what He has done, our weary hearts
are uplifted and strengthened. From time to time every Christian
needs this kind of encouragement.

Are you tired? Are you discouraged with the way life is going?
Does the goodness of God sometimes seem only to be an empty

OUR STORIES
OF GRATITUDE

INWARD STRENGTH
AND JOY

Fig. 12.3. The Result of Gratitude

theoretical concept? Expressing gratitude in prayer can help. By telling God our stories of gratitude we can come to know in a deep and personal way that God is good to us here and now. Our souls can find the joy and peace of seeing God's loving, tender hand at work in our lives (see fig. 12.3).

In this chapter we have explored several dimensions of gratitude in prayer. We have seen the purpose of thanksgiving. We have also noted how to tell God stories of what He has done for us. The result of such expressions is a special measure of strength and joy in Christ. Effective communication of gratitude to God is an essential part of every fruitful prayer life.

Discussion Questions

1. What is the basis and purpose of showing gratitude in prayer? How do we often miss this dimension of prayer?

2. How may our prayers contain stories of gratitude?

3. What results can we expect for our lives when we devote ourselves to showing gratitude in prayer?

Exercises

1. Tell a story to someone about a series of events that demonstrate

God's blessing in your life. Reflect on how this story can be related to some biblical story.

2. Write a six-to-eight-sentence prayer in which you tell a story of gratitude to God. Also include a summary of some biblical event of which your story reminds you. Follow the form below as much as possible.

Lord, You are _____
(description of God)

_____.

We recall how You have blessed us so much _____

_____
(Recite a story of gratitude.)

_____

_____.

These events remind us of _____
(Summarize a relevant biblical story.)

_____

_____

_____

_____.

We thank You with all our hearts for Your endless mercy. Amen.

Extended Exercise

This week take the opportunity to pray at least twice, including a story of gratitude for God's blessing. You may find the form of exercise 3 helpful.

13

More Than Words

O bless the Lord, my soul;
Let all within me join,
And aid my tongue to bless his Name,
Whose favors are divine.

Isaac Watts
1674-1748

People use more than mere words to communicate. We convey messages through our tone of voice, our facial expressions, and even our body positions. One day a visitor stopped by my office. He said he just wanted to chat for a while, but I soon perceived that he was deeply troubled. While we exchanged pleasantries, he sat upright with his eyes fixed on the floor, his right hand rubbing back and forth against his left. When I asked him what was wrong, he confessed that he was heavy-hearted. Our chat immediately turned to a rather long discussion about some significant problems. Most of us have been in similar situations. We listen to words that communicate part of a message but also notice other signs that communicate more than words.

Likewise, communicating with God entails much more than putting words together. Christians often think that prayer is simply a matter of using proper terminology and putting standard ideas in an acceptable verbal format. But communication in prayer entails much more. God pays attention to the inflection of our voices, our expressions, our posture, and other forms of body language. In this chapter we will explore these nonverbal dimensions of prayer. How does

God want us to speak to Him with more than words?

Weeping and Singing

In Scripture, when people pray, they are not detached from their words. Their prayers are deeply personal and arise from within their souls. As a result, many biblical prayers display strong feelings. Frequently these attitudes are communicated through spoken words much like most of our modern prayers. Yet, in some circumstances, mere words will not suffice. In such instances, other modes of speech are available to us. For example, prayer may often involve weeping and singing.

Shedding tears in prayer is an important dimension of many psalms. When the psalmists turned to God in times of anguish, they often wept as they prayed. In Psalm 39:12 we read,

> Hear my prayer, O LORD,
>   listen to my cry for help;
>   be not deaf to my weeping.

The psalmist is in terrible anguish as he faces the world around him. Out of that sense of need he weeps bitterly before God. Psalm 6 also illustrates the appropriateness of weeping while in prayer. The psalmist calls out to God for help, saying:

> My soul is in anguish.
> How long, O LORD, how long? (v. 3).

His foes have troubled him so long that he says:

> I am worn out from groaning;
>   all night long I flood my bed with weeping
>   and drench my couch with tears.
> My eyes grow weak with sorrow;
>   they fail because of all my foes (vv. 6-7).

Throughout the Bible weeping is part of communication with God in times of sorrow and mourning. When the people of God suffer severely, they cry before Him. As they face obstacles that are too great for them, they weep. The display of sadness and intense need through weeping is a vital dimension of prayer.

A number of years ago I was involved with a group of Christians, many of whom were former drug abusers. Our members had their ups and downs, but one young man stood out in my mind as a prime example of a person radically transformed by Christ. Upon becoming a believer he turned completely around and fled from drugs altogether. One Sunday afternoon, nearly a year after his conversion, my friends and I received a phone call from the young man's mother. She was frantic. Apparently he had taken a drug and run out of the house in a violent rage.

The news hit hard. We were distressed that our brother had stumbled back into his former life, but the situation was serious for another, more deadly reason. A few days earlier, word had reached us that a bad mix of heroin had hit the streets of our city. Apparently a dealer had cut the drug with a poison. Immediately, the same fear seized all of us. What if our friend had used the contaminated drugs?

We all knew that this situation was far beyond our ability to handle, so we went to God in prayer. As we knelt before God, we began to express our fears so intensely that before long we all began to cry. Words decreased as tears increased, and we wept bitterly.

After our time of prayer, I drove home, still sad and disappointed over the events of the day. Then, unexpectedly, I spied our friend walking along the side of the highway. I stopped and picked him up. Happily, God had answered our prayers. He had not obtained his drugs from the contaminated source. After a few days he was much better and on his way to a full recovery. In that time of anguish, we communicated in prayer with more than words. We opened our hearts with weeping, and God heard our cry.

Children in many modern cultures, especially little boys, are taught that tears are a sign of weakness. "Grown men don't cry," we are told. One regrettable effect of this perspective is the discomfort we feel about weeping in prayer. Our prejudice against such displays of emotion runs so high in some circles that crying is seen as a lack of faith in God. These opinions, however, run counter to many biblical examples of prayer. Therefore, we must rid ourselves of this cultural straitjacket. We must learn that, at times, only by

bathing our words with tears can we adequately express our hearts
to God.

The Scriptures make it plain that God pays special attention to the
weeping of His children. God saw the tears of Hezekiah and said:

> I have heard your prayer and seen your tears; I will heal you.
> On the third day from now you will go up to the temple of the
> LORD (2 Kings 20:5b).

We can be assured that God will never overlook our tears:

> Record my lament;
> list my tears on your scroll—
> are they not in your record? (Ps. 56:8).

Just as human parents are drawn sympathetically toward the tears
of their children, God looks on us with mercy as we weep before
Him. God has called us to communicate with Him. One vital dimension of this communication is the ability to weep in prayer.

Just as we may express sorrow through weeping, we may also
communicate our joy to God by singing to Him. The people of God
originally sang or chanted most of the prayers of the Psalms. In
Psalm 9:1-2, for instance, we read:

> I will praise you, O LORD, with all my heart;
> I will tell of all your wonders.
> I will be glad and rejoice in you;
> I will sing praise to your name, O Most High.

In this light, the words of James become clear:

> Is any one of you in trouble? He should pray. Is anyone happy?
> Let him sing songs of praise (James 5:13).

Singing in prayer is a vital part of communication with God.

Happily, we have many good resources for this aspect of prayer.
Most Christian hymnals contain songs that were written as prayers.
Many traditional hymns are explicitly directed to God, even though
Christians seldom sing them with the conscious intention of com-
municating with God.

I enjoy taking long walks by myself. They afford me an escape

Fig. 13.1. Modes of Speech

from distractions and an opportunity to be alone with God. I remember one evening not long after I had become a Christian, when I was walking along a trail in the Blue Ridge Mountains of Virginia. As I rounded a turn, I caught sight of one of the most beautiful sunsets I had ever seen. Standing there before God's beautiful artistry, I began to pray. But my prayer did not consist of mere words. I began to sing the familiar hymn "Holy, Holy, Holy." At first I felt a bit strange. Suppose someone came from behind and heard me singing to myself? Then I realized for the first time that I was not singing to myself. This song was a prayer of thanksgiving and praise directed to God. So, I stood in the woods all alone singing at the top of my voice to God. By singing, I communicated much more than I could ever have said with mere words. The zeal of my heart broke through as I lifted that melody. Offering a song in the midst of prayer can greatly enhance conversation with God.

The mode of speech we adopt in prayer will significantly affect our communication with God. Mere words will not suffice in many situations. Often we need to pray, weeping and singing (see fig. 13.1).

Kneeling and Lifting Hands

In recent years the importance of body language has become a focus of scientific research. These studies have demonstrated that people communicate with each other through facial expressions, gestures, posture, and other bodily movements. Counselors and psychologists are trained to spot the subtle messages body language sends. Often how people sit, fold their arms, and focus their eyes reveals attitudes they would never express in words. Body language can also be an important dimension of communication with God. We will focus on two of the more prominent ways of communicating through posture: kneeling and lifting hands in prayer.

Kneeling was a well-known custom in the ancient world. People of lowly estate were expected to bow in the presence of royalty. To bend the knee or to lower the head was an expression of humility and respect for the person of higher rank. Everyone knew that refusal to do so was the height of defiance and rebellion.

Bowing before superiors was such a part of the ancient world that it is no wonder the Bible stresses this posture for worship and prayer. God is the supreme Monarch, and we are His lowly, creaturely servants. As His inferiors we dare not enter His presence with arrogance. We must come with humility and reverence. This is why we read in the familiar call to worship,

> Come, let us bow down in worship,
> let us kneel before the LORD our Maker (Ps. 95:6).

This passage clearly associates worship with kneeling before God. Why? Because worship is a matter of revering and honoring God.

Notice Solomon's posture as he prays at the dedication of the temple:

> Now he had made a bronze platform, five cubits long, five cubits wide and three cubits high, and had placed it in the center of the outer court. He stood on the platform and then knelt down before the whole assembly of Israel and spread out his hands toward heaven (2 Chron. 6:13).

We find an explicit reference to kneeling in Psalm 44:25:

> We are brought down to the dust;
> our bodies cling to the ground.

When believers of old turned to God in prayer, they knew their true condition as creatures and sinners. So they demonstrated their humility by bowing as they offered their entreaties.

The example of the prophet Daniel stresses the importance of kneeling before God. Daniel's political rivals had convinced King Darius to issue a decree commanding everyone to pray only to the king himself (Dan. 6:1-9). Daniel easily could have hidden the fact that he continued to pray to God by simply praying in his heart as he walked down the street or sat in his home. But he did not. Instead Daniel knelt down to pray as usual:

> Now when Daniel learned that the decree had been published, he went home to his upstairs room where the windows opened toward Jerusalem. Three times a day he got down on his knees and prayed, giving thanks to his God, just as he had done before (Dan. 6:10).

The prophet was so convinced of the importance of kneeling in humility before God that he bowed down even though it endangered his life.

These examples from Scripture stand in stark contrast to the practices of many believers today. Many Christian churches and organizations seldom, if ever, encourage their participants to kneel as they pray. This neglect is often a reaction to liturgical forms of worship that require kneeling. We must be careful, however, not to overreact to what we may view as empty ritual. Kneeling and bowing in prayer is a biblical imperative. It stimulates attitudes of humility and reverence in our hearts and allows us to express those attitudes to God.

Once I went to visit a local pastor whose reputation as a Bible teacher was great. We spent some time talking about my conversion to Christ and how my life had been changed. Then, as the conversation came to an end, he invited me to pray with him. Much to my surprise, he rose from his chair, came to my seat, and knelt down with his face to the ground. At first, I was shocked, but I quickly joined him on my knees. Here was a man who had plenty of reason for self-confidence, but he demonstrated a heart of reverence toward God by bowing before Him in prayer. His example that day has never left my mind. Whenever I am tempted to take prayer lightly, I remember this pastor. Kneeling to pray expresses a devotion and reverence for God that goes far beyond any words we may say. It is a practice all Christians should embrace.

Another prominent form of body language that Scripture enthusiastically endorses is lifting hands. We have already seen how Solomon combined kneeling before God with lifting his hands toward heaven (2 Chron. 6:13). Not only the Old Testament but also the New Testament commands this practice:

> I want men everywhere to lift up holy hands in prayer, without anger or disputing (1 Tim. 2:8).

For many Christians this prayer ritual is an enigma. What did believers in biblical times hope to communicate when they raised their hands?

On the one hand, the Psalms indicate that lifting hands to God in prayer is a way of expressing great joy. In Psalm 63:3-4, we read:

> Because your love is better than life,
>   my lips will glorify you.
> I will praise you as long as I live,
>   and in your name I will lift up my hands.

Notice the level of happiness and excitement these few lines reveal. The blessings of God so overwhelm the psalmist that he proclaims that God's faithfulness is better than life itself. To express this attitude to God, he says he will glorify God (v. 3), praise Him (v. 4), and lift up his hands (v. 4). The same theme occurs throughout the Psalms. Consider Psalm 134:2:

> Lift up your hands in the sanctuary
>   and praise the LORD.

Raising hands to God is the psalmists' way of enthusiastically communicating praise to Him. It is as if we take our thanksgiving into our hands and raise it as an offering to heaven. Gratitude stirs our hearts and puts words on our lips, but we can also communicate this attitude through the physical expression of raising our hands toward God.

On the other hand, this form of prayerful body language can also express a sense of intense need. As one psalmist puts it:

> To you I call, O LORD my Rock;
>   do not turn a deaf ear to me.
> For if you remain silent,

I will be like those who have gone down to the pit.
Hear my cry for mercy
    as I call to you for help,
as I lift up my hands
    toward your Most Holy Place (Ps. 28:1-2).

It is apparent from these lines that the psalmist has a great need. If God does not answer his plea, he will soon be like a dead man (v. 1). So he cries for mercy and entreats God by lifting his hands toward the place of His presence (v. 2).

We see a similar portrait in Psalm 143:6-7a:

I spread out my hands to you;
    my soul thirsts for you like a parched land.

Answer me quickly, O LORD;
    my spirit faints with longing.

The psalmist's soul longs for the mercy of God as dry ground yearns for water. How is this longing expressed? Not in mere words. His cries for help are accompanied by a lifting of the hands. Just as raised hands can symbolize giving praise to God, they can also give physical expression to our hearts begging for help from God. We lift our hands heavenward with the hope that God will fill them, as it were, with His rich blessings.

Having seen that kneeling and lifting hands are biblically warranted postures for prayer, we must take a step back and assess the practice of believers today. Since many churches and Christian organizations have neglected these practices, we must begin to reaffirm the value of body language in prayer. Still, we must also exercise caution. Severe disharmony can result when a small group becomes enthusiastic about kneeling or lifting their hands in public meetings. These well-mean believers can disrupt worship services and eventually create all sorts of problems within a church. We should never hesitate to take full advantage of all the avenues of communication with God in private. Yet, if kneeling or lifting hands in a public worship service is disruptive, we should limit the practice to our private times of prayer. In corporate worship we must be concerned not only with our own edification but also with the building up of the whole body. Spiritual exercises should not be practiced in public

POSITIONS
EXPRESSIVE
OF
ATTITUDES

Fig. 13.2. Body Language in Prayer

if they benefit only a few. Nor should we exercise freedoms that severely disrupt the worship experiences of others. Out of respect for our brothers and sisters, we should remember the words of Paul:

> All of these must be done for the strengthening of the church (1 Cor. 14:26b).

Whatever the case, believers must not entirely neglect these physical forms of communication with the Lord. God has ordained kneeling and lifting hands as important parts of prayer. As we bow before God, we express our humility and reverence for Him. As we lift our hands, we display our praise and our intense need. When these patterns become our practice, we can find ourselves moving further into effective communication with God (see fig. 13.2).

Fasting and Prayer

When I was in college, I worked at night as a home nurse. I sat up all night with an elderly man who was suffering from brain cancer. During the six months I worked there, I grew to love the ailing man and his wife. They had no children, and I soon began to fulfill the role of a son. One wintry night the man became extremely weak. His

breathing grew erratic and soon stopped entirely. He passed away
that same night at three o'clock in the morning. This was the first
time I had ever seen someone die. I remember the fear, the grief, and
the dread that gripped me as I went to tell his wife that her lifelong
companion had passed away.

As that day dragged on, I continued to feel the loss. "Life is so
fragile, so short," I thought to myself. During the next day I helped
in every way I could. The day of the funeral service, however, I began
to feel ill. I wondered what was wrong, and then I realized that in my
grief I had not eaten since that dreadful night. My heart was so
preoccupied by the event that I had set food aside. Somehow eating
and going through this kind of loss simply did not go together.

This common human experience illustrates some of the basic
ideas involved in the biblical practice of fasting. In our modern
world, people fast for numerous reasons. Some groups claim that it
helps mental alertness to abstain periodically from food. Some try to
lose weight quickly by fasting. In the Bible, however, fasting is a
religious rite. It is the voluntary self-denial of food or drink for the
purpose of expressing to God our intense concern and preoccupation with something.

Biblical fasting occurs in many different contexts. The death of a
loved one was one occasion for fasting in the Bible:

> Then David and all the men with him took hold of their clothes
> and tore them. They mourned and wept and fasted till evening
> for Saul and his son Jonathan, and for the army of the LORD
> and the house of Israel, because they had fallen by the sword
> (2 Sam. 1:11-12).

At the death of a family member or friend, biblical figures expressed
their grief and their yearning for God's comfort through fasting.

Second, a fast demonstrated heartfelt repentance over sin and the
urgent desire for forgiveness. Upon hearing the preaching of Jonah,
the city of Nineveh responded with fasting:

> The Ninevites believed God. They declared a fast, and all of
> them, from the greatest to the least, put on sackcloth
> (Jonah 3:5).

Similarly, Ezra fasted because of the sins of Israel:

Then Ezra withdrew from before the house of God and went to
the room of Jehohanan son of Eliashib. While he was there, he
ate no food and drank no water, because he continued to
mourn over the unfaithfulness of the exiles (Ezra 10:6).

Third, the people of God fasted when they faced problems or
tasks that required extraordinary help from God. When foreign
invaders threatened Jerusalem, Jehoshaphat declared a fast:

Alarmed, Jehoshaphat resolved to inquire of the LORD, and he
proclaimed a fast for all Judah (2 Chron. 20:3).

Similarly, when Esther decided to risk her life on behalf of her
people, she requested a fast:

Go, gather together all the Jews who are in Susa, and fast for
me. Do not eat or drink for three days, night or day. I and my
maids will fast as you do. When this is done, I will go to the
king, even though it is against the law. And if I perish, I perish
(Esther 4:16).

In these settings, fasts provided an opportunity for intense supplication in prayer.

Fourth, fasting also occurred as part of self-examination and
preparation for meeting with God:

On the tenth day of this seventh month hold a sacred assem-
bly. You must deny yourselves and do no work (Num. 29:7).

Preparing to meet with God was an awesome event, which de-
manded thorough evaluation of oneself and urgent yearning for
God's blessing.

In all of these different situations, fasting expressed various kinds
of intense concern and religious devotion to finding God's blessing
in times of need.

The church today must face a terrible reality. We have virtually
lost the art of fasting. On the American scene, only a handful of
denominations practice it with any regularity. Few individuals devote themselves to periods of fasting as a normal part of their
spiritual development.

This neglect has had terrible consequences. We have cut ourselves off from many wonderful prayer experiences. Because we ignore fasting, we are plagued with an inability to grieve effectively before God. We labor under the burden of loss and sadness far longer than is necessary. Without fasting, we tend to express repentance over serious sins with superficial sentence prayers. How can we demonstrate deep sorrow over flagrant violations of God's holy law without fasting? Beyond this, Christians today also have no vehicle for setting aside periods of time to concentrate heavily on intense needs. Fasting has been given for such times. In all these cases, valuable dimensions of the Christian life have vanished because we have forgotten how to fast.

In my years as a Christian, I have served in a number of Christian organizations. Each organization, at one time or another, has faced very serious problems. Sometimes these problems were far beyond the ability of leadership to handle. We formed committees and spent hours discussing matters. But rarely did anyone suggest a fast. In fact, of all the organizations I have served, only one made it a practice to deal with serious problems through prayer and fasting. If believers in the Bible found fasting valuable, how can modern Christians continue to ignore it? I am convinced that much of the frustration we experience as Christians is the result of not taking advantage of the practice of fasting.

When crucial events occur, we should be ready to fast. The disciples of John the Baptist once questioned Jesus about the lifestyles of His disciples and He responded:

> How can the guests of the bridegroom mourn while he is with them? The time will come when the bridegroom will be taken from them; then they will fast (Matt. 9:15).

Jesus said in no uncertain terms that after His departure to heaven, His disciples would fast. If we want to communicate with God in ways that reveal deep need and yearning for Him, we must make fasting a part of our lives. In fasting, we have a wonderful opportunity to communicate our deepest and most intense sense of devotion to God (see fig. 13.3).

In this chapter we have seen that communication in prayer goes far beyond words. We may express ourselves through weeping or singing. We may demonstrate our attitudes through kneeling and

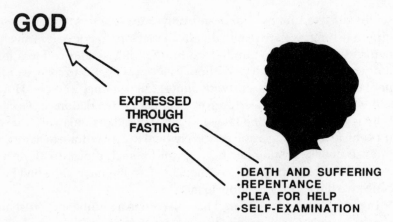

Fig. 13.3. Purposes of Fasting

lifting our hands. We may enhance our prayers through the practice of fasting. As we make these elements a vital part of our prayers, our communication with God will be more effective and rewarding than ever before.

Discussion Questions

1. Why do we often hesitate to weep and sing in prayer? How can we overcome our inhibitions in these areas?

2. Why is body language a valuable part of prayer? What positions for prayer are taught in the Bible? How can we begin to use body language in prayer?

3. What are the purposes of fasting? How can our communication with God be enhanced through fasting?

Exercises

1. Name an event in your life in which you wept. Also describe an event in which you caught yourself singing joyfully. Why were mere spoken words not adequate in these circumstances? How can these insights be applied to prayer?

2. Discuss the pros and cons of different positions (kneeling, lifting hands, standing, sitting, etc.) in prayer. In what circumstances should you experiment with expressing your heart through kneeling and lifting hands?

3. Write a four-to-five-sentence prayer that would be appropriate for kneeling or lifting hands. If possible, read your prayer in that position. As much as possible, use the following form as a guide.

O _____ , we
                    (name or title for God)

worship You now as we (bow on our knees/lift our hands). With our bodies we demonstrate what is in our hearts. You deserve our worship because _____
                    (Describe something about God that expresses your worshipful attitude.)

_____

_____

_____ .

We humble ourselves and acknowledge how we need You. You alone can _____
                    (Describe some things you need that God alone can provide.)

_____

_____ .

Hear our prayer and look upon us with mercy as we seek You, O Lord. Amen.

Extended Exercise

Three times this week pray in a kneeling position about something that requires a humble heart. Then end your prayer by singing a hymn with uplifted hands. You may also wish to prepare for one of these times of prayer by fasting for one or two meals.

14

Practicing Prayer

Little Jim wanted to play football. His heart was set on becoming a professional player. "I'm smart enough to do it," he thought to himself. Actually, Jim was quite a bookworm. He read all the time and knew exactly what to do to become a famous football star—or so he thought. "I'll check out some books from the library and find out everything about this game," he said to his younger sister on their way to school. Several weeks later the first day of tryouts came. After warm-up exercises, the coach shouted, "Tackle practice!" When Jim reached the front of the line, he scrambled for the boy with the ball but to no avail. Once, twice, three times the runner easily avoided Jim's frantic attempts to bring him down. Finally, the coach called Jim off to the side. "Jim," he whispered, "I just don't think you're cut out for football." "Oh yes I am," he retorted. "Ask me anything about the game. I know the answer to any question you can ask." The coach knelt down and put his hand on Jim's oversized shoulder pad. "Jim, in football it's not what you *know*. It's what you *do* that counts."

Now that we've come to the end of this study, I want to make a few personal comments on putting these chapters into practice. As

Jim wanted to play football, I'm sure you desire a fruitful prayer life. We have spent many pages exploring prayer from the perspectives of God, ourselves, and our communication. Perhaps you have learned a thing or two. But that just isn't enough. In prayer it's not what you *know*. It's what you *do* that counts.

Good communication with God is not something developed simply by reading. You can read a thousand books on the subject without improving your prayers in the least. Prayer is like learning to play football or the piano. It takes practice. Our prayer lives will develop only as we take time to put our good intentions into action.

Prayer may be put into practice in countless ways. In my own experience, two particular areas have been especially important.

Private Prayer

One matter we all must take seriously is the value of private prayer. Few things in life are as precious as time spent alone with God. But nothing is easier to neglect.

From the example of Daniel, we can see that believers should spend time in prayer every day (Dan. 6:10). Yet, many Christians struggle to make regular daily prayer a part of their lives. Who wants to take time out of a busy day for something as boring as most of our personal devotions? So we must look for ways to enliven our daily private prayers.

Sometimes focusing on one or two of the topics in the preceding chapters brings the vitality we need. One day, try spending time on God's character and another day on His actions. Instead of always going through the same list or following the same unwritten pattern, fill one morning prayer with nothing but praise. Spend another time in nothing but lament. Whatever the case, concentrating on the various dimensions of prayer will greatly enhance daily communication with God.

As important as regular daily prayers are, we should also occasionally spend more lengthy times alone with God. Jesus' withdrawal to the wilderness in preparation for His ministry illustrates how He periodically sought seclusion to be alone with God (Matt. 4:1).

When was the last time you took a day or two to get away from it all—not to take a vacation but to be alone with God? For many Christians such a practice is unimaginable. But what could be more reasonable when we have a difficult decision to make? What could be more profitable when we are discouraged? What could be more essential when life seems out of control? Times of personal retreat devoted entirely to God should be a part of every Christian's experience.

But how is it possible to spend a whole day in prayer? What could a person do all that time? If it is planned well, a day of seclusion and communion with God can be a magnificently rewarding experience. Many believers find it helpful to plan a comprehensive schedule for a day of prayer. One suggestion is to work with units of thirty minutes. Try spending the first half-hour with a particular focus on one or more of the elements in the preceding chapters (praise, lament, God's attributes, His actions, etc.). Take the next period to sing related hymns and psalms. Use the third thirty-minute segment for Scripture reading. Finally, devote the last period to rest or a quiet walk. Then the cycle may begin again (see fig. 14.1).

Whatever schedule suits you best, it has been my experience that planning is crucial. A schedule of activities will make the day such a wonderful blessing that you will wonder where all the time went.

These are just a few ideas to consider. Regular and special times of private communication with God are rich opportunities for God's children to be with their heavenly Father. I hope you will renew your vigor in regular communion and special times of solitude with God.

Corporate Prayer

While prayer is a very private experience, it is also to be shared in community. We are called to communicate with God corporately as well as individually. As the people of God, we participate in many associations. We are members of families, circles of friends, special organized ministries, local churches, regional associations, denominations, and the visible church throughout the world. Throughout the Bible believers prayed together. From small groups to large

TWO-HOUR CYCLE

- **PRAYER WITH A PARTICULAR FOCUS (30 MIN.)**
- **SING HYMNS AND PSALMS (30 MIN.)**
- **SELECTED SCRIPTURE READING (30 MIN.)**
- **QUIET REST (30 MIN.)**

Fig. 14.1. Schedule for a Personal Retreat

national assemblies, corporate prayer has always been vital to God's people. Today, many well-meaning believers think that prayer is so personal that they do not need to involve themselves in public prayer. This outlook denies many of us access to one of the richest sources of encouragement and strength available in this life.

Although regular corporate prayer times are essential, it is very easy for them to become lifeless. I have been in countless churches where the prayer meeting is run exactly the same way week after week. It is no wonder that most members do not attend. The splendor of group prayer is reduced to an ordeal of endurance by the constant repetition of the very same uninteresting patterns.

Do you want to enliven your regular times of corporate prayer? One of the most helpful practices I have seen is to plan special emphases for these meetings. In some circumstances, a particular illness or problem in the church can be the focus of an entire meeting. At other times, it may be appropriate to celebrate a special holiday through prayer. In this book many different patterns and focal points are presented, which can be incorporated into group prayer meetings.

Another area that many organizations and church groups need to work on is special times of corporate prayer. It has been my experience that leadership retreats and meetings may be *called* "prayer retreats," but they are usually filled primarily with discussions and planning. Frankly, I wonder if we should stop planning so much and begin to pray more. We need to come to the point where pastoral staffs and councils of Christian organizations spend a day or two each year solely in prayer. This is how inner strength is built into a group. This is how we invoke God's lasting blessing on our organizations.

Once again, however, planning is important. When a group is not

LARGE GROUP MEETING (45 MIN.)
  (SCRIPTURE, EXHORTATIONS, SONGS, PRAYERS, SILENCE)
SMALL GROUPS (45 MIN.)
  (SPECIFIC PRAYER ASSIGNMENTS)
LARGE GROUP (45 MIN.)
  (SINGING, PRAISES, THANKSGIVINGS)
QUIET REST (45 MIN.)

Fig. 14.2. Schedule for Special Corporate Prayer Times

accustomed to this kind of lengthy prayer, it is crucial to have variety. No particular plan will suit every organization, but we must make an effort to make these meetings vital. One approach is for the whole group to meet for a forty-five-minute session for brief instructions, singing, unison prayers, and silent preparation. Then break into small groups with specific prayer assignments for another forty-five minutes. The next period may be spent together in singing and testimonies, followed by a time of quiet rest. As time allows, this pattern may be repeated again and again (see fig. 14.2).

Corporate prayer times present many challenges. If we enhance these times by careful preparation, they can become essential threads in the fabric of every Christian organization.

So it is that we must go beyond learning about prayer. Nothing short of practicing prayer will do. Talking with God is an essential dimension of our private and corporate Christian experience.

With these few suggestions we must close this study of prayer. We began with an honest recognition of the problems we have in this area. Although we have only begun to explore this vast subject, we have looked at several avenues by which we may improve our communication with God. May God richly bless you as you continue to discover what it means to *pray with your eyes open*.

Appendix A
Names, Titles, and Metaphors for God

This appendix contains a number of the names, titles, and meta-phors for God the Father, Son, and Holy Spirit within the Bible. Some are paraphrased slightly for more convenient listing. The variety exhibited here should encourage us to address God in many ways in our prayers (see chap. 2).

God the Father

Abba, Father—Mark 14:36; Rom. 8:15; Gal. 4:6
Ancient of Days—Dan. 7:9, 13, 22
Creator—Isa. 27:11; 40:28
Creator of Israel—Isa. 43:15
Father—Luke 11:2
Father-Creator—Mal. 2:10
Father of Compassion—2 Cor. 1:3
Father of Glory (NASB)—Eph. 1:17
Father of Lights (NASB)—James 1:17
Father of Our Spirits—Heb. 12:9
God—Gen. 1–2:3 (*"Elohim"*)
God Almighty—Gen. 17:1-2; 48:3-4; 49:25; Ps. 91:1 (NIV: "God, Almighty")
God Most High—Gen. 14:18-22; Ps. 78:56; Dan. 4:25; Num. 24:16; Acts 7:48
God of Abraham, Isaac, and Jacob—Exod. 3:6, 16
God of Heaven and Earth—Ezra 1:2; 5:11; Neh. 1:4; Rev. 11:13

God of Hope—Rom. 15:13
God of Israel—Gen. 33:20
God of Justice—Mal. 2:17
God of Peace—Heb. 13:20
God Our Father—Eph. 1:2
God the Father—2 Tim. 1:2; 2 Pet. 1:17
Holy Father—John 17:11
Holy One—Isa. 43:15; Hab. 3:3
Jealous—Exod. 20:5; 34:14; Deut. 4:24
Judge of the Earth—Gen. 18:25; Ps. 94:2
King—Pss. 10:16; 74:12; 84:3; Isa. 43:15
King of Glory—Ps. 24:7-10
King of Heaven—Dan. 4:37
King of the Ages—Rev. 15:3
King of the Nations—Jer. 10:6-7
Living God—Dan. 6:20, 26; Matt. 16:16; Rom. 9:26
Lord of All the Earth—Josh. 3:11, 13; Mic. 4:13; Zech. 6:5
Lord of Lords—Deut. 10:17
Lord Our Righteousness—Jer. 23:5-6; 33:16
Lord, the God of the Hebrews—Exod. 7:16
Our Father—Matt. 6:9
Redeemer—Job 19:25; Isa. 47:4
Righteous Father—John 17:25
Rock—Deut. 32:4, 15; Ps. 18:2
Rock of Israel—Gen. 49:24
Savior—Hos. 13:4
The Faithful God—Deut. 7:9; 32:4
The Father—1 John 1:2; 3:1; 4:14
The First and the Last—Isa. 48:12
The God of All Comfort—2 Cor. 1:3
The God of Daniel—Dan. 6:26
The God of Gods—Deut. 10:17
The God of the Armies of Israel—1 Sam. 17:45
The God Who Sees—Gen. 16:13
The Great and Awesome God—Neh. 1:5
The Lord Is My Banner—Exod. 17:15
The Lord Is Peace—Judg. 6:24
The Lord Is There—Ezek. 48:35

The Lord My God—Josh. 14:8; Ezra 7:28; Pss. 7:1; 18:28; 30:2; Zech. 14:5

The Lord My Shepherd—Gen. 48:15; 49:24; Ps. 23

The Lord of Hosts (NASB)—1 Sam. 1:3; 4:4; 17:45; Isa. 6:3; 47:4; Hag. 2:4,6

The Lord Our God—Deut. 1:6, 19, 20; 2:29, 33; 3:3; 4:7; 6:4

The Lord Our Maker—Ps. 95:6

The Lord Who Heals—Exod. 15:26

The Lord Who Sanctifies (NASB)—Exod. 31:13; Lev. 20:7-8; 21:8, 15, 23

The Lord Will Provide—Gen. 22:14

The Mighty One of Jacob—Gen. 49:24

Yahweh—Gen. 4:26; Exod. 6:2-3; Num. 14:18; Ps. 106:25. Also: LORD, Jehovah

Your Father—Matt. 5:16; John 20:17

God the Son

Advocate (NASB, KJV)—1 John 2:1-2

Alpha and Omega—Rev. 1:8; 22:13

Apostle and High Priest—Heb. 3:1

Author and Perfecter—Heb. 12:2

Author of Salvation—Heb. 2:10

Blessed and Only Ruler—1 Tim. 6:15

Branch From Jesse—Isa. 11:1

Bread of God—John 6:33

Bread of Life—John 6:35

Bridegroom—Matt. 25:1-10; Mark 2:19-20; John 3:29

Chosen of God—Luke 23:35; 1 Pet. 2:4

Chosen One—Isa. 42:1; Luke 23:35

Christ Jesus Our Lord—2 Tim. 1:2

Christ of God—Luke 9:20; 23:35

Christ the Lord—Luke 2:11

Christ, the Power of God and the Wisdom of God—1 Cor. 1:24

Consolation of Israel—Luke 2:25

Cornerstone—Isa. 28:16; 1 Pet. 2:6

Deliverer—Rom. 11:26

Desired of All the Nations—Hag. 2:7
Everlasting Father—Isa. 9:6
Faithful and True—Rev. 19:11
Faithful and True Witness—Rev. 3:14
First Born—Heb. 1:6
First Born From the Dead—Col. 1:18; Rev. 1:5
Firstborn Among Many Brothers—Rom. 8:29
Firstborn Over All Creation—Col. 1:15
Forerunner (NASB)—Heb. 6:20
Foundation—1 Cor. 3:11
Fountain—Zech. 13:1
Friend—Matt. 11:19
Gate—John 10:7-9
Gift of God—John 4:10
Glory of Israel—Luke 2:32
Good Shepherd—John 10:11, 14
Head of the Church—Eph. 5:23; Col. 1:18-20
Heir of All Things—Heb. 1:2
High Priest—Heb. 3:1; 4:14; 7:26-27
Holy One—Acts 2:27
Holy One of God—Mark 1:24; Luke 4:34; John 6:69
Hope of Glory—Col. 1:27
Horn of Salvation—Luke 1:69
I Am—John 8:58
Immanuel—Matt. 1:23; Isa. 7:14
Jesus—Matt. 1:21; Acts 9:5; Heb. 2:9
Jesus Christ—Matt. 1:1
Jesus of Nazareth—Mark 1:24; John 18:5, 7; 19:19
Judge—Acts 10:42
King—Luke 19:38
King of Kings—1 Tim. 6:15; Rev. 19:16
Lamb—Rev. 5:6
Lamb of God—John 1:36
Light of the Gentiles—Luke 2:32
Light of the World—John 8:12; 9:5
Lion of the Tribe of Judah—Rev. 5:5
Living Stone—1 Pet. 2:4
Lord—Matt. 22:43-44; Mark 1:3; Luke 7:13; Rom. 10:9; Phil. 2:11

Lord and Savior Jesus Christ—2 Pet. 1:11; 2:20; 3:18
Lord of Glory—1 Cor. 2:8
Lord of Lords—1 Tim. 6:15; Rev. 19:16
Lord of the Dead and Living—Rom. 14:9
Lord of the Sabbath—Matt. 12:8; Mark 2:28
Master—Matt. 23:8
Mediator—1 Tim. 2:5; Heb. 12:24
Messiah—John 1:41; 4:25
Mighty God—Isa. 9:6
One and Only—John 1:14, 18; 3:16
Our Holiness—1 Cor. 1:30
Our Passover—1 Cor. 5:7
Our Redemption—1 Cor. 1:30
Our Righteousness—Jer. 23:6; 1 Cor. 1:30
Physician—Luke 4:23
Prince—Acts 5:31
Prince of Life—Acts 3:15
Prince of Peace—Isa. 9:6
Rabbi—Mark 10:51; John 1:38, 49
Rabboni—John 20:16
Radiance of God's Glory—Heb. 1:3
Redeemer—Isa. 44:24; Gal. 4:5
Righteous Branch—Jer. 23:5
Righteous Judge—2 Tim. 4:8
Righteous One—Acts 7:52; 1 John 2:1
Righteous Servant—Isa. 53:11
Rising Sun—Luke 1:78
Rock—1 Cor. 10:4
Root and Offspring of David—Rev. 22:16
Root of David—Rev. 5:5
Ruler—Mic. 5:2; Matt. 2:6
Ruler of God's Creation—Rev. 3:14
Savior—Luke 2:11; Acts 5:31; 1 Tim. 2:3; Titus 3:6
Second Man—1 Cor. 15:47
Servant—Isa. 52:13-15; Phil. 2:7
Shepherd and Overseer—1 Pet. 2:25
Son—Col. 1:13; Heb. 3:6
Son of Abraham—Matt. 1:1

Son of God—Matt. 8:29; 14:33; John 10:36
Son of Man—Matt. 8:20; Mark 2:10; John 1:51; 3:13
Son of the Blessed One—Mark 14:61
Son of the Father—2 John 3
Son of the Living God—Matt. 16:16
Son of the Most High God—Mark 5:7; Luke 8:28
Stone—Matt. 21:42; 1 Pet. 2:8
Sure Foundation—Isa. 28:16
Teacher—John 13:14
The Almighty—Rev. 1:8; 15:3
The Amen—Rev. 3:14
The Beginning—Col. 1:18
The Branch of the Lord—Isa. 4:2
The Christ—John 7:41; Acts 2:36
The Last Adam—1 Cor. 15:45
The Life—John 11:25; 14:6
The Morning Star—2 Pet. 1:19; Rev. 22:16
The Prophet—John 7:40
The Resurrection—John 11:25
The Son of God—Matt. 8:29; Mark 1:1; Luke 1:35; John 10:36;
    Acts 9:20
True God—1 John 5:20
True Light—John 1:9
True Vine—John 15:1
Truth—John 14:6
Way—John 14:6
Wisdom—1 Cor. 1:30
Wonderful Counselor—Isa. 9:6; see also Isa. 28:29
Word—John 1:1, 14
Word of God—Rev. 19:13

God the Holy Spirit

Breath of the Almighty—Job 32:8; 33:4
Counselor—John 14:16
Deposit—Eph. 1:13-14
Eternal Spirit—Heb. 9:14

God—Acts 5:3-4
God's Seed—1 John 3:9
Good Spirit—Neh. 9:20
Helper (NASB)—John 14:16, 26; 15:26; Rom. 8:26
His Holy Spirit—1 Thess. 4:8
His Spirit—Ps. 106:33; Eph. 3:16; 1 John 4:13
Holy Spirit—Matt. 1:18; Mark 12:36; John 1:33; Acts 4:8; Rom. 15:16
Holy Spirit of God—Eph. 4:30
Living Water—John 7:38-39
Lord—2 Cor. 3:17-18
Power of the Most High—Luke 1:35
Promise of the Father—Acts 1:4; 2:33
Seal—Eph. 4:30
Seven Spirits—Rev. 1:4-5; 4:5; 5:6
Spirit—Num. 11:17, 25, 26
Spirit He Gave Us—1 John 3:24
Spirit of Christ—Rom. 8:9; 1 Pet. 1:11
Spirit of Counsel—Isa. 11:2
Spirit of Faith—1 Cor. 12:9; 2 Cor. 4:13
Spirit of Fire—Isa. 4:4
Spirit of Glory—1 Pet. 4:14
Spirit of God—Gen. 1:2; Job 33:4; Matt. 3:16; 12:28
Spirit of Grace and Supplication—Zech. 12:10
Spirit of Him Who Raised Jesus From the Dead—Rom. 8:11
Spirit of His Son—Gal. 4:6
Spirit of Holiness—Rom. 1:4
Spirit of Jesus—Acts 16:7
Spirit of Jesus Christ—Phil. 1:19
Spirit of Judgment—Isa. 4:4
Spirit of Knowledge—Isa. 11:2
Spirit of Life—Rom. 8:2
Spirit of Our God—1 Cor. 6:11
Spirit of Power—Isa. 11:2
Spirit of Promise—Eph. 1:13
Spirit of Sonship—Rom. 8:15
Spirit of the Fear of the Lord—Isa. 11:2
Spirit of the Living God—2 Cor. 3:3
Spirit of the Lord—Isa. 11:2; Luke 4:18; Acts 8:39; 2 Cor. 3:17

Spirit of the Lord God—Isa. 61:1
Spirit of Truth—John 14:17; 15:26; 16:13
Spirit of Understanding—Isa. 11:2
Spirit of Wisdom—Isa. 11:2
Spirit of Wisdom and Revelation (NASB)—Eph. 1:17
Spirit of Your Father—Matt. 10:20
Spirit Who Intercedes for Us—Rom. 8:26-27
Spirit Who Is From God—1 Cor. 2:12
Spirit Who Searches All Things—1 Cor. 2:10
Your Holy Spirit—Ps. 51:11

Appendix B
The Attributes of God

The following list of divine attributes is designed as an aid for focusing on the character of God in prayer. It is often helpful to read the biblical passages noted and to incorporate them in prayer. This list is highly selective but provides a number of vital perspectives on the character of God (see chap. 3).

Incommunicable Attributes*

Independent
(Self-existent)
". . . he does whatever pleases him" (Ps. 115:3; cf. John 5:26; Rom. 11:35-36).

Infinite
". . . from everlasting to everlasting . . ." (Ps. 90:1-2; cf. Pss. 33:11; 93:2; 145:13; Heb. 1:8-12).

Eternal
". . . the LORD, the Eternal God" (Gen. 21: 33; cf. Neh. 9:5-6; John 8:58; Rev. 1:8).

Incomprehensible
". . . beyond our understanding" (Job 36: 26; cf. Isa. 40:18-26; Matt. 11:27; Rom. 11: 33-34).

Supreme
(Pre-eminent)
". . . all things were created by him and for him . . ." (Col. 1:15-19; cf. Exod. 15:1, 11, 18; Rev. 19:11-16).

*Qualities that belong to God alone.

Sovereign   "I will do all that I please . . ." (Isa. 46:10;
                            cf. Ps. 135:6; Dan. 4:35; Eph. 1:11).

Transcendent   ". . . beyond our reach . . ." (Job 37:23;
                            cf. Exod. 33:20-23; Ps. 104:1-4; Isa. 40:21-
                            26; 1 Tim. 6:15-16).

The One and Only   ". . . there is but one God . . ." (1 Cor. 8:
                            6; cf. Deut. 6:4; Isa. 45:21-22; 1 Tim. 2:5).

Majestic   "In the greatness of your majesty . . ."
                            (Exod. 15:7; cf. 15:6, 11; Job 37:22; Ps. 8:1, 9;
                            Jude 25).

Present Everywhere   "Do not I fill heaven and earth?" (Jer. 23:
   (Omnipresent)   23-24; cf. 2 Chron. 2:6; Ps. 139:7-16; Acts
                            17:27-28).

All-Knowing   ". . . you alone know the hearts of all men
   (Omniscient)   . . ." (1 Kings 8:39; cf. Ps. 139:1-6; Prov. 3:
                            19-20; 1 Cor. 2:10).

All-Powerful   "Is anything too hard for the LORD?"
   (Omnipotent)   (Gen. 18:14; cf. 1 Sam. 2:6-7; Ps. 18:13-15;
                            Rev. 19:6).

Unchanging   ". . . you remain the same . . ." (Ps. 102:
   (Immutable)   27; cf. Mal. 3:6; James 1:17; Heb. 13:8).

Communicable Attributes*

Holiness   "Your ways, O God, are holy" (Ps. 77:13;
                            cf. Isa. 6:3; 57:15; 1 Pet. 1:15-16; Rev. 4:8).

Wisdom   ". . . magnificent in wisdom" (Isa. 28:29;
                            cf. Jer. 10:12; 1 Cor. 1:30; Col. 2:2-3).

Truthfulness   ". . . God is truthful" (John 3:33; cf. Num.
   (Veracity)   23:19; Isa. 45:19; John 14:6).

*Qualities that belong to God and can be reflected in us through the work of the
Holy Spirit.

Love	". . . his unfailing love . . ." (Ps. 33:5, 18, 22; cf. Exod. 15:13; Pss. 13:5-6; 89:2; Rom. 8:38-39; Eph. 3:17-19; 5:1-2).
Goodness	"He is good" (2 Chron. 7:3; cf. Gen. 1:31; Pss. 119:68; 145:9; Mark 10:18).
Faithfulness	". . . he is the faithful God . . ." (Deut. 7:9; cf. Pss. 33:4; 100:5; 1 Cor. 1:9; 1 Thess. 5:24).
Mercy	". . . his mercy is great . . ." (2 Sam. 24:14; Neh. 9:31; Dan. 9:9; Luke 1:50, 54).
Kindness	". . . he shows unfailing kindness . . ." (2 Sam. 22:51; cf. Isa. 54:8; Jer. 9:24; Rom. 11:22).
Patience (Forbearance, Long-suffering)	". . . his unlimited patience . . ." (1 Tim. 1:16; cf. Neh. 9:30; Rom. 3:25; 2 Pet. 3:15).
Justice	". . . all his ways are just . . ." (Deut. 32:4; cf. Job 37:23; Ps. 99:4; Luke 18:7-8).
Righteousness	". . . my righteousness will never fail" (Isa. 51:6; cf. Ps. 89:14; Jer. 23:5-6; 1 Cor. 1:30).
Wrath	". . . expresses his wrath every day" (Ps. 7:11; cf. Deut. 29:28; Isa. 13:13; Rom. 1:18; 5:9; 9:22; Rev. 19:15).
Jealousy	". . . a jealous God" (Exod. 34:14; cf. Deut. 4:24; Nah. 1:2; Zech. 8:2; 2 Cor. 11:2).
Grace	". . . God, gracious and compassionate . . ." (Neh. 9:17; cf. Exod. 34:6-7; Isa. 26:10; 2 Tim. 1:9; Titus 3:5-7).

Index of Scripture